OPPOSING VIEWPOINTS® SERIES

Genetic Engineering

Other Books of Related Interest:

Opposing Viewpoints Series

Cloning

At Issue Series

Adaptation and Climate Change

Designer Babies

Genetically Engineered Food

Should Parents Be Allowed to Choose the Gender of Their Child?

Global Viewpoints

Genetic Engineering

Introducing Issues with Opposing Viewpoints

Global Warming

Stem Cell Research

"Congress shall make no law . . . abridging the freedom of speech, or of the press."

First Amendment to the US Constitution

The basic foundation of our democracy is the First Amendment guarantee of freedom of expression. The Opposing Viewpoints series is dedicated to the concept of this basic freedom and the idea that it is more important to practice it than to enshrine it.

OPPOSING VIEWPOINTS® SERIES

Genetic Engineering

Noël Merino, Book Editor

GREENHAVEN PRESS
A part of Gale, Cengage Learning

GALE
CENGAGE Learning

Detroit • New York • San Francisco • New Haven, Conn • Waterville, Maine • London

GALE
CENGAGE Learning

Elizabeth Des Chenes, *Director, Publishing Solutions*

For more information, contact:
Greenhaven Press
27500 Drake Rd.
Farmington Hills, MI 48331-3535
Or you can visit our Internet site at gale.cengage.com

Articles in Greenhaven Press anthologies are often edited for length to meet page requirements. In addition, original titles of these works are changed to clearly present the main thesis and to explicitly indicate the author's opinion. Every effort is made to ensure that Greenhaven Press accurately reflects the original intent of the authors. Every effort has been made to trace the owners of copyrighted material.

LIBRARY OF CONGRESS CATALOGING-IN-PUBLICATION DATA

Genetic Engineering (Merino)
Genetic engineering / Noël Merino, book editor.
pages cm. -- (Opposing viewpoints)
Includes bibliographical references and index.
ISBN 978-0-7377-6424-6 (hardcover) -- ISBN 978-0-7377-6425-3 (pbk.)
1. Genetic engineering--Juvenile literature. 2. Human reproductive technology--Juvenile literature. 3. Food--Biotechnology--Juvenile literature. I. Merino, Noël, editor of compilation. II. Title.
QH442.G4535 2013
576.5--dc23

2012044960

Printed in the United States of America
1 2 3 4 5 6 7 17 16 15 14 13

Contents

Why Consider Opposing Viewpoints? 11

Introduction 14

Chapter 1: Should Genetic Engineering Be Permitted?

Chapter Preface 18

1. Genetic Engineering Is Natural and Should Be Pursued 20
Jeffrey Scott Coker

2. The Three Mile Island of Biotech? 33
John Nichols

3. Human Genetic Engineering Should Be Allowed 46
Ronald M. Green

4. We Must Stop Trying to Engineer Nature 53
Mark Lynas

5. Stem Cell Research Should Be Allowed, but Not Reproductive Cloning 57
Barack Obama

6. Ignored Implications 63
Ken Blackwell

Periodical and Internet Sources Bibliography 68

Chapter 2: What Are the Benefits and Risks of Genetic Engineering?

Chapter Preface 70

1. Genetically Modified Foods Could Pose Numerous Health Risks 72
Institute for Responsible Technology

2. Genetically Modified Foods Have Numerous Benefits and No Known Risks 79
Henry I. Miller

3. Genetically Modified Crops Can Increase Productivity to End World Hunger 85
Erik Vance

4. Genetically Modified Crops Will Not Increase Productivity to End World Hunger 92
Union of Concerned Scientists

5. Preventing the Next Fertility Clinic Scandal 101
Jesse Reynolds

6. Society Could Benefit from Allowing Unregulated Embryo Trait Selection 108
Greg Beato

Periodical and Internet Sources Bibliography **114**

Chapter 3: What Is the Environmental Impact of Genetic Engineering?

Chapter Preface **116**

1. Human Genetic Engineering Is a Good Solution to Climate Change 119
S. Matthew Liao, interviewed by Ross Andersen

2. Human Genetic Engineering Is a Dangerous Proposal to Combat Climate Change 129
Mark Tapson

3. Genetically Engineered Fish Can Provide Food and Conserve the Planet 134
Yonathan Zohar

4. Genetically Engineered Pigs Could Provide Environmental Benefits 140
Anne Minard

5. Genetically Engineered Pigs Are Not a Good Solution to Environmental Problems 145
Lucy Sharratt

Periodical and Internet Sources Bibliography 152

Chapter 4: How Should Genetic Engineering Technology Be Regulated?

Chapter Preface 154

1. New Genetic Engineering Technology Needs to Be Regulated 157
Richard Hayes

2. New Genetic Engineering Technology Does Not Need to Be Regulated 163
Ronald Bailey

3. Knowing Me, Knowing You 170
Jeanne Lenzer and Shannon Brownlee

4. Consumer Genetic Testing Does Not Need Additional Regulation 181
Christopher Mims

5. The US, the UN and Genetic Engineering 187
Chuck Norris

6. Labeling of Genetically Modified Foods Is Unnecessary and Unconstitutional 192
Henry I. Miller and Gregory Conko

Periodical and Internet Sources Bibliography 198

For Further Discussion 199

Organizations to Contact 201

Bibliography of Books 207

Index 211

Why Consider Opposing Viewpoints?

> *"The only way in which a human being can make some approach to knowing the whole of a subject is by hearing what can be said about it by persons of every variety of opinion and studying all modes in which it can be looked at by every character of mind. No wise man ever acquired his wisdom in any mode but this."*
>
> *John Stuart Mill*

In our media-intensive culture it is not difficult to find differing opinions. Thousands of newspapers and magazines and dozens of radio and television talk shows resound with differing points of view. The difficulty lies in deciding which opinion to agree with and which "experts" seem the most credible. The more inundated we become with differing opinions and claims, the more essential it is to hone critical reading and thinking skills to evaluate these ideas. Opposing Viewpoints books address this problem directly by presenting stimulating debates that can be used to enhance and teach these skills. The varied opinions contained in each book examine many different aspects of a single issue. While examining these conveniently edited opposing views, readers can develop critical thinking skills such as the ability to compare and contrast authors' credibility, facts, argumentation styles, use of persuasive techniques, and other stylistic tools. In short, the Opposing Viewpoints Series is an ideal way to attain the higher-level thinking and reading skills so essential in a culture of diverse and contradictory opinions.

In addition to providing a tool for critical thinking, Opposing Viewpoints books challenge readers to question their own strongly held opinions and assumptions. Most people form their opinions on the basis of upbringing, peer pressure, and personal, cultural, or professional bias. By reading carefully balanced opposing views, readers must directly confront new ideas as well as the opinions of those with whom they disagree. This is not to argue simplistically that everyone who reads opposing views will—or should—change his or her opinion. Instead, the series enhances readers' understanding of their own views by encouraging confrontation with opposing ideas. Careful examination of others' views can lead to the readers' understanding of the logical inconsistencies in their own opinions, perspective on why they hold an opinion, and the consideration of the possibility that their opinion requires further evaluation.

Evaluating Other Opinions

To ensure that this type of examination occurs, Opposing Viewpoints books present all types of opinions. Prominent spokespeople on different sides of each issue as well as well-known professionals from many disciplines challenge the reader. An additional goal of the series is to provide a forum for other, less known, or even unpopular viewpoints. The opinion of an ordinary person who has had to make the decision to cut off life support from a terminally ill relative, for example, may be just as valuable and provide just as much insight as a medical ethicist's professional opinion. The editors have two additional purposes in including these less known views. One, the editors encourage readers to respect others' opinions—even when not enhanced by professional credibility. It is only by reading or listening to and objectively evaluating others' ideas that one can determine whether they are worthy of consideration. Two, the inclusion of such viewpoints encourages the important critical thinking skill of objectively evaluating an author's credentials and bias. This evaluation will illuminate an author's reasons for taking a particular stance on an issue and will aid in readers' evaluation of the author's ideas.

It is our hope that these books will give readers a deeper understanding of the issues debated and an appreciation of the complexity of even seemingly simple issues when good and honest people disagree. This awareness is particularly important in a democratic society such as ours in which people enter into public debate to determine the common good. Those with whom one disagrees should not be regarded as enemies but rather as people whose views deserve careful examination and may shed light on one's own.

Thomas Jefferson once said that "difference of opinion leads to inquiry, and inquiry to truth." Jefferson, a broadly educated man, argued that "if a nation expects to be ignorant and free . . . it expects what never was and never will be." As individuals and as a nation, it is imperative that we consider the opinions of others and examine them with skill and discernment. The Opposing Viewpoints series is intended to help readers achieve this goal.

David L. Bender and Bruno Leone,
Founders

Introduction

> *"Genetic engineering enables people to introduce a much wider range of new traits into an organism than is possible by conventional breeding."*
>
> *US Food and Drug Administration*

Genetic engineering is the process of deliberately modifying genes, also known as gene splicing, gene manipulation, or recombinant DNA (deoxyribonucleic acid) technology. The modification of genes entails manipulating the DNA of organisms at the molecular level, using recombinant DNA techniques; that is, techniques that recombine genes. Enzymes are used to remove or add pieces of DNA, altering, adding, or deleting genes. Often, the genes from one organism are removed and inserted into another organism. The products of genetic engineering are becoming common throughout the world. Pharmaceuticals for humans have been produced using genetically engineered bacteria. Gene therapies are being developed to treat human disease. Food eaten by people and animals has been genetically modified.

One of the first genetically engineered products was a genetically engineered form of insulin. Developed in the 1970s, the process isolates the gene for producing human insulin protein and puts it in the DNA of a bacterium. The bacterial cell produces insulin and those human insulin protein molecules are gathered and purified. Millions of people now take this form of genetically modified insulin to treat their diabetes.

Research on the use of genetic engineering to treat disease is under way, often involving experimental use, on humans with various medical conditions. The US Food and Drug Administration (FDA) has not yet approved any gene therapy product for sale, but it is in charge of the oversight for clinical trials. Several widely publicized failures of gene therapy clinical trials have raised red flags about the process. Teenager Jesse Gelsinger died in 1999 four days after starting gene therapy treatment for ornithine transcarbamylase deficiency (OTCD). In 2005, the FDA halted several gene therapy trials after three boys treated by gene therapy for X-linked severe combined immunodeficiency (X-SCID) developed cancer. And in 2007, the FDA stepped in to halt a clinical trial using a gene therapy for inflammatory arthritis after one of the participants died. Clinical trials continue, but there are concerns about using gene therapy for nonfatal diseases, given the possible risks.

Genetically engineered food is now widespread in the United States. The first commercially genetically engineered food to gain acceptance by the FDA was the Flavr Savr tomato, which was developed by combining the genes of a tomato with the *E. coli* bacterium to create a gene that was able to delay the softening and rotting of the tomato. The resulting Flavr Savr tomatoes were too delicate to transport and were also reportedly bland in flavor, causing this particular genetically engineered crop to leave the market in 1997. Several crops, including canola, soybeans, and corn, now are frequently genetically modified and have had better commercial success than the Flavr Savr tomato. Over 90 percent of canola and over 80 percent of both soy and corn grown in the United States are genetically modified. Due to concerns about the safety of such products, many consumer groups argue for better labeling and information about what foods contain genetically modified ingredients.

In the 1980s the gene for bovine somatotropin (BST)—a cow hormone that regulates milk production—was cloned and injected into the *E. coli* bacterium. This allowed the bacteria to grow along with the engineered cow hormone recombinant bovine somatotropin, or rBST. The hormone is harvested and purified, and then used to increase milk production in dairy cows. The FDA approved rBST in 1993, and many dairy farmers began using the genetically engineered growth hormone. The use of rBST has been controversial from the start and is now banned for use in Canada and the European Union. Nonetheless, the FDA, World Health Organization (WHO), American Medical Association (AMA), and the National Institutes of Health have independently stated that dairy products and meat from BST-treated cows are safe for human consumption.

The science of genetic engineering is advancing rapidly, and the number of products with manipulated genes is likely to grow in coming years. The technology holds promise for disease treatment and for foods that can adapt to changing conditions globally. Nonetheless, debate is still rampant about the safety and efficacy of the use of genetic engineering, and many questions emerge regarding the wisdom of moving forward with this technology, as noted in this volume's chapters: Should Genetic Engineering Be Permitted?, What Are the Benefits and Risks of Genetic Engineering?, What Is the Environmental Impact of Genetic Engineering?, and How Should Genetic Engineering Technology Be Regulated? Answers to these questions from a variety of perspectives are explored in *Opposing Viewpoints: Genetic Engineering*, shedding light on this fascinating and complicated contemporary issue.

OPPOSING VIEWPOINTS® SERIES

CHAPTER 1

Should Genetic Engineering Be Permitted?

Chapter Preface

Public opinion on the use of genetic engineering varies widely depending on the goal of the technology. Opposition to genetic modification lessens when the technology is used for the treatment of human disease. Additionally, the use of genetic engineering in plants is less opposed than the use of genetic engineering in animals and humans, with most Americans willing to consume genetically engineered plants. Thus, it is not the technology itself that is often opposed but particular uses of the technology.

In a 2012 Gallup poll, 86 percent of respondents said that cloning humans was morally wrong and 60 percent said that cloning animals was morally wrong. A 2010 Virginia Commonwealth University (VCU) Life Sciences Survey found similar results, with 58 percent strongly opposing the use of cloning technology in humans and 22 percent somewhat opposed to it. In this survey, a majority of people, 58 percent, agreed that "scientific research these days doesn't pay enough attention to the moral values of society." However, the same survey found that when asked whether they favored cloning when it is limited to helping develop new treatments for disease, only 40 percent opposed it. This illustrates that public opinion on the use of genetic engineering varies depending on what the technology is used to accomplish.

The genetic engineering of plants results in less opposition than the genetic engineering of animals. A 2010 Thomson Reuters poll found that 60 percent of Americans are willing to eat vegetables, fruits, or grains that have been genetically engineered. Yet, only 38 percent would eat genetically engineered meat, and only 35 percent would be willing to consume genetically engineered fish. Regardless of willingness to consume genetically engineered food, a vast majority believes that these foods should be labeled, with 93 percent saying that any food with genetically engineered ingredients should indicate this to the consumer.

Public opinion of the various types of genetic engineering will surely evolve as the technology advances and as more facts become known about potential risks and rewards. The viewpoints in this chapter present varying opinions on whether genetic engineering—including stem cell research and cloning—should be permitted.

"Genetic engineering is actually as natural as any process on Earth, and mastering it would enable us to do what microbes do trillions of times every day, but purposefully and with better results."

Genetic Engineering Is Natural and Should Be Pursued

Jeffrey Scott Coker

In the following viewpoint, Jeffrey Scott Coker argues that genetic engineering is a promising technology for agriculture and humans. Coker claims that despite public outcry over genetic engineering, scientists widely support its use. He contends that genetic engineering currently in use has solved agricultural problems and created lifesaving medicines for humans. Coker concludes that future human manipulation of genes is natural and desirable. Coker is assistant professor of biology at Elon University in North Carolina.

As you read, consider the following questions:

1. According to Coker, more than what percentage of soybeans, cotton, and corn in the United States are already genetically engineered?

Jeffrey Scott Coker, "Crossing the Species Boundary: Genetic Engineering as Conscious Evolution," *Futurist*, vol. 46, no. 1, 2012, pp. 23–37.

2. According to the author, what was the first drug for human health produced by genetic engineering?
3. The author predicts that what genetic enhancement already used in mice and monkeys might be the first to be used on humans?

Gene mutation is far more common and more natural than some people may think. Although we tend to think of ourselves as genetically stable entities, the truth is that every one of us mutates multiple times every day. Every time one of our cells duplicates itself, a couple of hundred DNA mutations occur. Since the human body has more than 10 trillion cells, that adds up to trillions of mutations, per person, over the course of a human life.

The Unfixed Nature of DNA

Viruses and bacteria routinely shuttle DNA between organisms in nature, so much of our DNA is nonhuman in origin. Biologists refer to this as "lateral gene transfer." Throughout evolutionary history viruses and bacteria have been shuttling DNA between organisms of every sort. Most commonly, they deposit their own DNA (which they are also passing readily among themselves). For example, one finding of the Human Genome Project was that humans have a substantial amount of bacterial DNA that was passed into humans through lateral gene transfer. Lateral gene transfer is a pretty common occurrence in nature, leading to the rapid spread of disease-resistance genes among microorganisms and other evolutionary events.

Once you realize that DNA is not fixed, and is in fact constantly changing, the notion of genetic engineering seems quite innocent. Changing DNA within an organism and transferring DNA from one species to another is not unprecedented, or even unusual. Microbes in nature are carrying it out every second.

The only thing truly new about genetic engineering is that it transfers control from microorganisms to humans, from randomness to consciousness. It is pretty difficult to argue that we should give random chance trillions of opportunities to change our DNA, but we shouldn't trust ourselves to do it even once. Humans have many faults, but we are not dumber or less trustworthy than random chance.

Scientists Support Genetic Engineering

The subject of genetic engineering often sparks an emotional reaction in many people. There is widespread support in some countries for banning genetic engineering, or at least imposing severe restrictions on it. Some activist groups have launched media campaigns and led mass protests against it. They express shock and outrage and denounce it as a "contaminant" and a "dangerous technology." A few groups of more militant demonstrators have gone so far as to vandalize research labs and sabotage experimental field trials.

Scientists attempt to view the issues surrounding genetic engineering more objectively. They foresee the technologies greatly benefiting humanity and the environment—as long as we proceed with caution. The Ecological Society of America has stated:

> Genetically engineered organisms have the potential to play a positive role in sustainable agriculture, aquaculture, bioremediation, and environmental management, both in developed and developing countries. However, deliberate or inadvertent releases of genetically engineered organisms into the environment could have negative ecological impacts under some circumstances.

The American Society of Plant Biologists firmly supports "responsible development and science-based oversight" of genetic engineering and states further that "with continued responsible regulation and oversight, genetic engineering will bring many significant health and environmental benefits to the world."

The National Academy of Sciences (NAS), which advises the U.S. government under congressional charter, reviewed the body of existing literature on crop production throughout the United States. In its 2010 report, NAS concluded that genetic engineering might not enhance agriculture everywhere, but it does significantly improve agriculture in many places and sectors.

The simplistic debate about whether or not genetic engineering is "right" or "wrong" is very unfortunate because it has distracted the public from the truly important questions about the future: How can we use genetic engineering to improve the world? How should the regulatory process be designed to maintain safety while still allowing the timely release of lifesaving therapies, improved crops, etc.? How can we utilize the benefits of genetic engineering without allowing a small number of corporations to dominate global agriculture? How can we use genetic engineering for humanitarian purposes? How can we use genetic engineering to cure cancer and other diseases? To what extent should genetic engineering be used for human enhancement?

Researchers in practically every major university and research institute are now thinking about these questions and using genetic engineering to help solve all sorts of global problems. It is no exaggeration to say that a revolution of innovation is taking place.

The Use of Genetically Engineered Crops

In the United States and elsewhere, more than 90% of soybeans, cotton, corn, and certain other crops are already genetically engineered, according to the U.S. Department of Agriculture. The most common genetic modifications involve increased defenses to insects and weeds. For example, "Roundup Ready" crops are immune to the herbicide glyphosate, allowing farmers to spray herbicide and kill weeds without harming the crop itself. (These crops are not without controversy, raising fears of corporate monopolization, indiscriminate spraying of toxic chemicals, etc.) Another example is "Bt" technology, which involves plants producing a protein from *Bacillus thuringiensis*, a bacterium that is toxic to most insects. Although these universal traits will persist, the next generation of genetically engineered crops will include traits for local adaptation, as well.

Many of the best applications for genetically engineered crops are local in nature—targeted solutions for specific problems. In Hawaii, for example, genetically engineered papaya trees have rescued the entire papaya industry. A ringspot virus was destroying all of Hawaii's papayas in the 1980s and 1990s. Researchers from Cornell University engineered a resistant tree that was then bred with other varieties. Now, more than 80% of Hawaiian papaya trees are immune to ringspot.

Similarly, on farms throughout China, farmers have been growing a cotton plant that is engineered to be resistant to the destructive pest cotton bollworm. Analysis has shown that these resistant cotton plants will even control the bollworm on nearby non-engineered plants.

Rice is a staple crop throughout the world, especially in poor areas. Researchers at the University of California-Riverside and the International Rice Research Institute have created varieties of rice that can withstand being submerged underwater for almost two weeks, which can save crops during years of flooding. At the University of California-Davis, rice has been engineered to have greater salt tolerance. Others are working on more nutritious rice that will be more resistant to drought, cold, iron toxicity, and other stresses. These new traits could have enormous humanitarian benefits.

Genetically Engineered Crops That Solve Problems

Colorado State University researchers have created plants that can change color when certain pollutants or explosives are nearby. This could allow the plants to serve as a warning system during a terrorist attack or industrial accident, or when land mines are left behind after wars.

Partial solutions to the world's energy needs are being addressed by genetic engineering as well. At many universities, organisms are being engineered with improved characteristics for producing biofuels (e.g., tolerance to glucose and ethanol). Plants, bacteria, yeast, algae, and other organisms have been engineered for this purpose.

In Australia, field trials have been promising for insect-resistant cotton, drought-tolerant and salt-tolerant wheat, and boron-tolerant and fiber-enriched barley. They have also created bananas that are fungus-resistant and fortified with vitamin A and iron.

In South Africa, researchers have engineered corn that is resistant to the maize streak virus. The virus, which is endemic to Africa, can destroy a farmer's entire crop in a bad year. Since corn accounts for more than 50% of calories consumed in some African regions, the new corn could help Africa to become more stable and self-sufficient.

We could go on and on with examples of genetic engineering being used to solve specific problems and improve particular crops. Basically, if you can imagine it, then several research labs are working on it. Genetic engineering will allow crops of the future to be better tasting, more nutritious, more tolerant of environmental stresses, and less allergenic. Foods will also last longer before spoiling, allowing food to be distributed more easily. Finally, and perhaps most importantly, there will be much more food grown per acre, meaning that we will need less land to grow crops. This creates the opportunity for millions of acres to remain wilderness instead of being leveled into farmland.

A Criticism of Genetic Engineering

A common criticism of engineered crops is that they allow a small number of large corporations to control an agricultural system. If every farmer is using the same genetically modified crops—particularly if they're from one manufacturer—then there will be less agricultural diversity, more corporate control, and little economic benefit for the farmers themselves.

In many situations, that has been partly true, but this is a problem that has to do with patenting and the regulatory system, not genetic engineering itself. As long as the regulatory environment is so biased against engineered crops, large companies will continue to dominate because most smaller players can't afford to get products approved. As with golden rice, many of the best uses of genetic engineering, especially those with benefits for poor and developing nations, are having trouble moving from the laboratory to the field.

To be fair, genetic engineering is not a panacea for agriculture and food supply. Agriculture is taking a serious toll on the planet. Global population is growing, soils are being degraded, and water supplies are being depleted. Perhaps most important, climate is changing, making traditional agricultural methods obsolete in many regions. Although genetic engineering can help remedy all of these problems, it cannot be a complete solution by itself. We will also need to embrace sustainable practices that build soils, reduce unnecessary herbicides and pesticides, increase biodiversity, reduce water usage, and distribute food more efficiently.

If we are wise, we will stop pitting different agricultural systems against one another. For example, both modern scientific farming and traditional indigenous agricultural systems have their place in the world. In a world with rapidly changing environments and cultures, we will need the tools and techniques of every agricultural system at our disposal to help individual regions cope with their own unique circumstances. Yesterday's techniques will not work when tomorrow's climate is so different. Likewise, using a small handful of corporate methods all over the planet is unlikely to benefit such a wide diversity of peoples and environments.

In my opinion, a sustainable and equitable future looks like this: Crops and livestock are genetically engineered with specific regions and peoples in mind, so that the local cultures are empowered and crop biodiversity is maintained. It is a world where ordinary people control their technology instead of the technology controlling them. This is the best future we can hope to attain.

Genetic Engineering in Drugs

Genetic engineering holds great potential importance for human health care as well. It can be used on other organisms to produce drugs, and it can also be used directly on humans to reverse harmful mutations.

The first drug produced by genetic engineering was insulin, approved by the U.S. Food and Drug Administration (FDA) in 1982. Before then, people with insulin-dependent diabetes had to inject themselves with insulin from cows or pigs. Although effective, cow and pig insulin increased the chances of allergic reactions. The company Genentech genetically engineered the bacterium *E. coli* so that it would produce a human version of insulin. Since this first success, genetic engineering has yielded therapies for multiple sclerosis, strokes, dwarfism, cancer, and a wide range of other diseases. By moving medicine away from using chemicals and parts derived from other animals and cadavers, genetically engineered products have resulted in higher success rates and fewer allergic reactions.

Genetic engineering is also invaluable as a method of disease prevention. Human papillomavirus (HPV) causes genital warts and is the main cause of cervical cancer, which kills hundreds of thousands of women each year. The pharmaceutical company Merck produces a widely used vaccine for HPV, which was among the first products to actually prevent a form of cancer. It is little known by the public that the vaccine is produced using genetically engineered yeast (and that is, in fact, the only way it could ever have been produced).

All around the world, companies are developing new genetically engineered drugs to fight cancer. Some will prevent forms of cancer outright, while others will help keep cancerous growth in check. For example, injecting tumor suppressor genes can slow some tumors.

Genetic Engineering to Fight Disease

Genetic engineering can also be used to fix genetic diseases, birth defects, and a broad range of other harmful mutations that occur "naturally" within human DNA. Most people don't like the sound of "engineering" humans. We don't think of ourselves as mechanical products, and we would much rather be "cured" than "engineered" or "fixed." With this in mind, many medical practitioners have adopted the gentler-sounding phrase "gene therapy," which includes a broad array of methods for using genetics to treat disease. Call it whatever you like, genetically based approaches are saving lives and restoring health.

For example, researchers from the University of Pennsylvania, Children's Hospital of Philadelphia, and University College London have corrected a gene defect in the eyes of people born with severe blindness and partly restored their sight. Only one injection of a liquid was needed to produce the dramatic results.

In another case, researchers at the National Institutes of Health genetically engineered the lymphocytes of cancer patients so that their cells would recognize and destroy cancerous cells. Several patients with rapidly advancing and deadly forms of cancer were cancer free a few months later. Yet another example is the treatment of HIV/AIDS. Many research groups are giving HIV-infected patients new genes to help fight HIV by removing blood or bone marrow, introducing new genes to immune cells, and then reinfusing the cells back into patients.

There are several thousand genetic diseases that are caused by DNA mutations and a variety of infectious diseases that use mutations of their own to outsmart our drugs. With genetic engineering, it may be possible to negate the vast majority of these genetic diseases and to develop much more effective, adaptable cures to the most mutation-prone pathogens. Thus, genetic engineering may become more and more important as a health care tool.

Extreme Forms of Genetic Engineering

It would be great fun to hop into a time machine and go back to witness the very first time that someone extracted and drank milk from a cow or goat. It must have seemed unthinkably disgusting to people at the time. Was it a caveman dare? Or a tribe who was desperately hungry? Or an early experimentalist?

Whatever the case, it goes to show that what seems extreme and unnatural to one generation or culture can be totally ordinary to the next. We eat and drink other organisms, even some that were once considered poisonous—tomatoes, for example. Likewise, ancient human cultures would have been shocked to hear that we now replace our organs with those from other animals, or graft plant species together to make them grow just as we like.

What are the more "extreme" genetic engineering projects of today that may seem ordinary tomorrow? Although genetically engineered animals are not yet a major part of agriculture, they are coming in a big way. They will be much more efficient—growing faster, requiring less food, and producing less waste. Eventually, they will also produce leaner, lower-fat meat.

If we choose, we could also grow meat in an industry setting that isn't really from an "animal," per se. The same cells that divide and grow to produce "meat" in an animal can be coaxed into growing synthetic meat in a laboratory. Some would argue that current meat production has become so miserable and unethical for animals that synthetic meat would be an ethical improvement. Public opinion will ultimately decide.

The Potential for Genetic Enhancement

In the realm of human health, genetic engineering will go far beyond treating acute health problems. We will see human enhancements of all sorts. Among the first could be people engineered to be slimmer and more muscular, both of which have already been accomplished in mice and monkeys. Eyesight could be greatly improved, perhaps even allowing us to see wavelengths of light that are currently "invisible" to us—maybe to the point where we might lessen our need for lighting and electricity use. Intelligence is more complicated and more impacted by one's environment, but it, too, could be genetically enhanced.

Undoubtedly, many people will protest vehemently at the notion of human enhancement, and some places will probably ban it. At the same time, though, the competitive pressures to use it will be enormous. Will the landscape of global power shift due to who embraces genetic technology and who doesn't? It is possible that we are in for a sort of genetic arms race or, if you view it more positively, a global revolution in genetic innovation. No matter what you call it, it would be an evolutionary sprint.

Genetic engineering will also very likely alter future athletic events. Unlike the use of performance-enhancing drugs, which a medical exam can detect, it will be nearly impossible to prove that an athlete underwent some types of genetic enhancement. In fact, some professional sports may be forced to allow every competitor access to essentially the same gene-altering technology. That way, at least they will have a level playing field. It is possible that we have already seen the last Olympic Games that are 100% free of genetically engineered athletic performance.

Some argue that genetic enhancement could ruin sports, and in some cases they may be right. On the other hand, was it ever really "fair" that a few people are lucky enough to be able to hit a baseball 450 feet, run 100 meters in under 10 seconds, or jump from the free throw line and dunk a basketball? Sports are already more dominated by genetics than we'd like to admit. The real decision is whether we prefer sports to be driven by genetic chance or genetic design. . . .

The Promise of Conscious Evolution

Once upon a time, our ancient ancestors scratched lives from nature. When food presented itself, they ate. When it did not, they starved. In the real world, "leaving nature alone" really means subjecting ourselves and our families to merciless and random suffering. Eventually, humans took more control of animals and plants through agriculture, and then civilization took off. Today, we can hardly imagine how harsh the preagricultural existence must have been.

Fast-forward to the future. Our descendants may look back at us in the same way that we look back at our ancestors. They will briefly consider what it was like for genetics to be random and uncontrolled, but they won't really understand. They will see us as poor wretches who struggled to do the best that we could under harsh circumstances. Just imagine one of your descendants strolling through a museum, looking at artifacts of the "pre–genetic engineering era," and wondering aloud, "What would it have been like to live during such a primitive time?" Just as today, some may not even believe that they evolved from us. "We couldn't have come from those monkeys," they may say.

Genetic engineering is actually as natural as any process on Earth, and mastering it would enable us to do what microbes do trillions of times every day, but purposefully and with better results.

Viewpoint 2

> *"The practical aspects of trying to keep these pharmaceutical plants separate from the regular food plants is an insurmountable problem. . . . It just can't be done. It can't be done because of the fallibility of human beings. It can't be done because you can't control pollen flow."*

The Three Mile Island of Biotech?

John Nichols

In the following viewpoint, John Nichols argues that the offspring of farm plants that have been genetically modified for the production of pharmaceuticals cannot be contained. He says that the inability to contain the genetically modified plants poses a threat to US agriculture and to humans. He further maintains that the open-air production and testing of the genetically modified plants has occurred without adequate regulation from the government or communication to farmers and consumers. Nichols is Washington correspondent for the Nation *and associate editor of the* Capital Times.

John Nichols, "The Three Mile Island of Biotech?," *The Nation*, December 12, 2002.

As you read, consider the following questions:

1. What biotech company took responsibility for covering the cost of the contaminated crops from Aurora, Nebraska, according to the author?
2. What are some of the scary results that could happen from mixing biopharmed crops with regular food crops, according to the viewpoint?
3. What do critics of the biotech industry say about the federal farm and environmental regulatory agencies, according to the viewpoint?

Hamilton County, Nebraska, is where food comes from. You can visit the Plainsman Museum on Highway 14 to learn about "farm life from the 1880s to the 1950s," or you can just drive on up the highway and learn about farm life in 2002 at any of the dozens of family farms that still grow corn and soybeans on fields that some families have worked since their ancestors homesteaded here just after the Civil War. For more than a century, farmers in this fertile stretch of a state where folks still refer to themselves as "cornhuskers" have planted food crops each spring and trucked the harvest in the fall to towering grain elevators on the edge of the bustling Great Plains town of Aurora. Those grains become the cereals, the breads, the cake mixes and the soy patties that feed America and the world.

This fall, however, the predictable patterns of Hamilton County and American food production took on the characteristics of a dystopian science-fiction story. An area farmer, who a year earlier had supplemented his income by quietly planting a test plot with seed corn genetically modified to produce proteins containing powerful drugs for treatment of diarrhea in pigs, this year harvested soybeans for human consumption from the same field. He trucked them off to the Aurora Co-op, where they were mixed with soybeans from other fields throughout the county in preparation for production as food. Just as the soybeans were about to begin their journey to the nation's dinner plates, a routine inspection of the test field by US Department of Agriculture inspectors revealed that corn plants that should have been completely removed were still growing in the field from which the soybeans had been harvested—raising the prospect that the pharmaceutical crop had mingled with the food crop.

Suddenly, as they say in Aurora, all kinds of hell broke loose. In November, USDA investigators swooped into town to order the lockdown of a warehouse filled with 500,000 bushels of food-grade soybeans that had been contaminated by contact with the beans containing remnants of the pharmaceutical corn. Aurora Co-op managers quietly secured the soybeans. But when word of the incident leaked out, Greenpeace campaigners climbed a tall white elevator to unfurl a banner that read: "This Is Your Food on Drugs!" Agitated officials of the Grocery Manufacturers of America expressed "concerns about the possible adulteration of the US food supply." Consumer groups made unfavorable comparisons between the incident in Hamilton County and the last great genetically engineered food debacle, which occurred two years ago when GE StarLink corn that had been approved solely for animal feed turned up in taco shells, chips and other food products.

Biotech industry groups and the government agencies with which they have worked closely to promote the increased use of genetically modified organisms in food crops rushed to assure consumers that all was well. Anthony Laos, CEO of ProdiGene, the Texas biotech company that has made Aurora ground zero for experiments in putting drugs into food, and that faced a possible $500,000 fine and the loss of its testing permit, promised to cover the $2.8 million cost of the contaminated crops. Jim Rogers, a spokesman for the USDA's Animal and Plant Health Inspection Service—which has been criticized for lax oversight of pharmaceutical crop experiments, commonly known as "biopharming"—said, "It's isolated, it's in one location, it's not being moved." That same week, however, it was revealed that ProdiGene had been ordered, just two months earlier, to burn 155 acres of corn from an Iowa field where stray biotech plants had "jumped the fence" and contaminated conventional corn crops.

But there is no two-strikes-and-you're-out rule at the USDA. ProdiGene got off with a $250,000 fine and a promise to follow regulations better. The company kept its permit to plant experimental crops, and biotech promoters continue to push for policies that could allow as much as 10 percent of US corn production to be devoted to pharmaceutical crops by 2010. "The future of biopharmaceuticals has simply never been brighter," said Laos. Farm and food activists worry that the events of fall 2002 will be little more than a bump in the road to the brave new world of biopharming.

"This is the Three Mile Island of biotech," says Mark Ritchie, president of the Institute for Agriculture and Trade Policy, comparing this fall's incidents to the near meltdown of the Pennsylvania nuclear power plant, which led to a dramatic shift in public attitudes about expansion of that industry. "The biotech industry says that because some soybeans were quarantined at the last minute, no one should worry. Well, at Three Mile Island, they contained things. But that didn't mean it wasn't a crisis, and it certainly didn't mean that people should have said, 'Oh, everything's fine now. Let's just let these guys get back to business as usual.'"

Ritchie says it's crucial to seize the moment—this is possibly the last chance to prevent the disasters that are all but certain to occur if biotech corporations are allowed to continue on their current course. "This is not the point to back off; this is the point to move very aggressively to get a handle on what is happening, and to control it," he says. "We're at the earliest stage of the attempt to genetically engineer corn plants to make them factories for producing powerful and potentially dangerous drugs, and already we have examples of contamination of food crops. This is scary stuff." [See Mark Schapiro, "Sowing Disaster?" October 28.]

How scary? Britain's Royal Society has expressed concerns about allergic reactions that could result from ingesting, inhaling or even touching biotech crops, while a new study by GE Food Alert, a coalition of health, consumer and environmental groups, details scientists' concerns about the prospect that eating crops containing biopharmaceuticals could weaken the immune system.

No one, not even the top scientists with the USDA, the Food and Drug Administration or the Environmental Protection Agency, can say with absolute certainty that the Iowa and Nebraska incidents are the only cases in which experimental pharmaceutical crops have jumped the fence from test plots and mixed with food crops. An expert committee of the National Academy of Sciences this year came to the conclusion that just as residue from more traditional GE cornfields has contaminated neighboring organic fields, so "it is possible that crops transformed to produce pharmaceutical or other industrial compounds might mate with plantations grown for human consumption, with the unanticipated result of novel chemicals in the human food supply."

The potential public health threat creates another threat—the health of American agriculture. Says Iowa State University agriculture professor Neil Harl, "If consumers take on the belief that corn products are being contaminated with products designed for vastly different uses—like HIV vaccines or hepatitis B vaccines or any of a variety of other things that are being discussed—and if they think this contamination poses a threat to them, that's going to create the risk of a negative reaction to corn grown in the United States. And consumers are kings. If consumers start to have doubts about US corn, farm-state economies are going to be in very serious trouble."

That prospect frightens Keith Dittrich, a corn farmer from north of Aurora who has shied away from offers to plant biopharm test plots. "This is being sold to farmers as a new specialty crop that could make them a lot of money," says Dittrich, the president of the American Corn Growers Association. "But if these experiments end up costing farmers markets in Europe or the United States, we could be looking at a short-term profit that turns into a long-term disaster." According to research by the ACGA, US corn farmers have already lost more than $814 million in foreign sales over the past five years as a result of restrictions on genetically modified food imports imposed by Europe, Japan and other countries.

"When it comes to what is being proposed, and what is actually happening with regard to genetic modification of food crops, we're absolutely navigating uncharted waters at a high rate of speed. And we're being pushed to speed up by people with dollar signs in their eyes and no concern whatsoever for farmers or consumers," says Nebraska Farmers Union president John Hansen. "There may be a television program here or an article there about what's happening, but I don't think most Americans have any idea of the extent to which things have been pushed forward without the kind of research and precautions that ordinary common sense would demand."

Biopharming represents the new frontier of biotechnology, where agribusiness meets the pharmaceutical industry to explore a once unimaginable prospect: manipulating the genetic code of plants to induce them to generate AIDS vaccines, blood-clotting agents, digestive enzymes and industrial adhesives. If their initiative works, the corporate promoters of biopharming predict, expensive laboratories and factories will by the end of this decade be replaced by hundreds of thousands of acres growing pharmaceutical corn and soybeans that will allow consumers to realize ProdiGene's promise that you can "Have Your Vaccine and Eat It, Too!" And those corpora-

". . . and if you want to get even with the place down the road, some tomato seeds with cactus genes could be blown onto their fields," cartoon by S. Harris, www.CartoonStock.com. Copyright © by S. Harris. Reproduction rights obtainable from www.CartoonStock.com.

tions will yield huge returns—ProdiGene predicts billion-dollar markets for products it has patented.

The dream of a biopharmed future is still presented as the noble cousin of GE cash-crop schemes. To the extent that Americans discuss genetic engineering, they usually refer to the process by which genes and segments of DNA that do not naturally occur in a particular food crop are added to it in order to make it easier, cheaper and more profitable to raise—such as the splicing of an antifreeze gene from flounder to produce a cold-resistant tomato. Biopharming pushes the limits of genetic engineering to a new plateau, where scientists re-engineer crops to produce drugs that can be extracted from kernels and beans far more cheaply than they can be produced in factories.

In their race to patent and market pharmaceutical crops, ProdiGene, Monsanto, Dow Chemical and various universities have quietly obtained permission from the USDA to have farmers plant open-air test plots across the United States; on these plots, the corporations are attempting—with some success—to turn corn, soybeans, rice and even tobacco into "plant pharmacies" that can provide edible vaccines for everything from hepatitis B to diabetes. Though biopharming is still in the experimental stage, the experiment has already seen twenty corporations and universities conduct more than 315 open-air field trials in undisclosed locations. These plots have brought thousands of acres—virtually all of them in the vicinity of fields growing traditional food crops—into biopharm production.

The race to the fields has sped up in recent years, in part because the biotech industry has many allies in the Bush administration and a Republican Congress that prefers "voluntary regulation" by industry to real regulation by the government. And these firms are actively recruited by state officials and university chancellors who believe that a biotech boom could turn Wisconsin or Iowa into a version of Silicon Valley. (ProdiGene was recruited to Texas during George W. Bush's governorship.) As a result, calls for limits on biopharming are often met with cries of "no way" from farm-state politicians.

"Nature is not a pharmaceutical factory. It was never meant to be. But we have reached the point where it may be possible to make it that, and that prospect excites politicians and corporate executives who see this as a new way to make money," says Bill Freese, a policy analyst with Friends of the Earth who wrote GE Food Alert's groundbreaking report on the dangers of manufacturing drugs and chemicals in traditional food crops. "They talk a great deal about the benefits for society. But it's really the economics that attract them. They think they can grow drugs more cheaply and have lower production costs than if they were produced in factories. Also, if a drug goes well, they can just scale up the acres involved in production. If the drug is a bust, they can just fire the farmers."

ProdiGene press releases describe the firm as being "well positioned to capitalize on the opportunities in the large and expanding recombinant protein markets." ProdiGene promotes itself as "the first . . . company to produce and market a recombinant protein product from transgenic plants," and it maintains a portfolio of ninety current and pending patents—including one to use plants to develop vaccines that can be eaten rather than injected. As a seed company and pharmaceutical industry executive, ProdiGene CEO Laos has for decades preached the bio-utopian "future of farming" gospel. To a greater extent than other biopharmers, he is determined to continue using corn as his company's preferred pharmaceutical plant. "We have looked at many different alternatives, and the best system available today for this technology is corn," he says.

And ProdiGene is getting lots of help. Its research on an edible AIDS drug is funded by the National Institutes of Health, and it recently developed a partnership with Eli Lilly. ProdiGene has collected more permits to initiate biopharm field trials than any other corporation in the United States—eighty-five, while the next most active experimenter, Monsanto, has just forty-four. Half of ProdiGene's permits are for fields in Iowa and Nebraska—the state that, according to the USDA, has been the site of the largest number of open-air field trials. And many of those fields are in Hamilton County, where Laos lived before taking charge of ProdiGene.

Laos has allies in the corn belt. In December, after the Nebraska and Iowa incidents, the Biotechnology Industry Organization (BIO) backed off a proposal to temporarily stop growing GE drug- and chemical-producing crops in major corn-growing states after the plan encountered noisy opposition from Iowa's Democratic Governor, Tom Vilsack, and other farm-state politicians, who still see biopharming as a boon. Many farmers in Hamilton County have planted test fields at the behest of seed salesmen associated with Laos and

ProdiGene. The salesmen offer small premiums—$600 for planting an acre of experimental corn and another $300 for managing it in the year after the experiment is done—along with the promise of bigger bonuses when the biotech train leaves the station. "They tell you: 'Once this gets going, the farmers who are in on it are going to make a lot of money growing these crops,'" says Mike Alberts, an Aurora-area farmer who this year turned down an opportunity to grow a ProdiGene test plot. "Farmers around here have had it hard for a long time, and a lot of them don't want to miss out on something they're calling the future of farming."

Critics of the biotech industry say that the federal agencies that should be strictly regulating burgeoning biopharm experimentation—the USDA, the Food and Drug Administration and the Environmental Protection Agency—are still too busy promoting GE crops as the cure for what ails American agriculture to recognize that they could turn into a curse. The USDA continues to hail GE crops as a boon for farmers, gleefully promoting biopharming with a website that features such headers as: "Animal Urine—A New Source of 'Pharmed' Medicine?" Even now, the agency allows agribusiness firms to withhold details about the nature of their experimental crops and the locations of test plots from the public—including neighboring food farmers—by declaring the data "Confidential Business Information."

"The regulatory system isn't working. It looks like we've got pharmaceutical chaos in the fields," says former North Dakota Agriculture Commissioner Sarah Vogel. "I'm not sure that some of these people in Washington or the corporate boardrooms quite understand the threat these incidents tell us are being created for food safety and the future of American agriculture." Part of the problem, according to Jean Halloran, who directs Consumers Union's Consumer Policy Institute, is that technological advances have outpaced not just regulations but basic questions of whether biopharming should be allowed at all. "What's infuriating is that there has been no public debate on whether we should be proceeding to this technology. They just went ahead and did it," Halloran says of an industry that, for the most part, is policed only with vague guidelines and threats of action if, as in the case of ProdiGene's plots, something goes really wrong. "We're in the middle of an official comment period on a set of guidelines—not regulations, just guidelines—at the same time that we are learning that we've got these problems with the testing. Doesn't that sound like we've missed a step?"

After the near disaster in Hamilton County, there may be some scaling back of the explosive growth in the number of biopharm test plots in corn-growing states. ProdiGene and USDA officials talk of "isolating" the firm's open-air test fields, just beyond the edge of the corn belt in Nebraska's Sand Hills or perhaps in the Southwest. But independent observers who know about farming and food safety are skeptical about this kind of self-regulation. They note that roughly 20 percent of the nation's corn production—including that of much of Nebraska—occurs outside the "drug-free zone" that BIO advanced and then abandoned. More significant, they argue that open-air test plots are not necessarily "isolated" by distance from traditional food crops.

Iowa State's Harl explains that even an isolated field can be hit with a tornado or heavy winds that will drop a kernel of corn far from the test plot. "Birds, deer, runoff from fields into rivers—it's hard to list all the ways that seeds and kernels can be carried substantial distances," says Harl, who adds that because of consumer confidence and liability concerns, "ultimately, I think we are going to conclude that we have to produce a zero-contamination rule. That requires us to control the total environment—and that means in a greenhouse."

Federal regulators have begun to feel pressure to tighten regulation of biopharm experiments and production, and not just from environmental, consumer and grocery industry groups, which have long been troubled by the prospect of drug crops contaminating food crops. In November Senate majority leader Tom Daschle and Agriculture Committee chair Tom Harkin wrote Agriculture Secretary Ann Veneman to ask "whether existing procedures and safeguards are sufficient to ensure that similar incidents do not occur in the future." A more energetic push came from the National Food Processors Association, whose president, John Cady, said the USDA and the FDA "should impose a stringent and mandatory regulatory framework to ensure protection of the US food supply and US food exports from any inadvertent or even intentional contamination by plant-made materials that have not been approved for human food and animal feed purposes." At the same time, however, farm groups allied with agribusiness—chief among them the American Farm Bureau Federation—issued a statement reaffirming their faith in biotech crops and essentially asking federal officials to continue encouraging biopharming.

Harl, who has served on the USDA's Advisory Committee on Agricultural Biotechnology, says federal agencies are going to have to fundamentally alter their approach to biopharming. "This is part of a broader regulatory phenomenon that has not been faced yet. If we are going to allow this type of production, then we have to ramp up the regulatory regimen," he says. The USDA, the FDA and the EPA must resolve turf wars over which agency is in charge of regulating not just test plots but, potentially, wide-scale production of pharmaceutical crops. That will require development of a regulatory regimen that makes public the details about where biopharm fields are planted and where biopharm products are being processed, and that insures regular testing through all the steps of food processing to assure that pharmaceutical crops are not being mixed with food crops. "We won't have discipline until we have testing at every point of commingling," Harl says. "We have some tests, but they are not what they must be: fast, easy and cheap."

Before any of these steps occur, however, Jean Halloran of Consumers Union suggests a more fundamental move. "We should ask whether pharmaceutical products should be engineered into food plants in the first place," she says. "Our view is that the answer to the question should be no." She notes that the drugs that biopharming promises to deliver can be gotten through other means. "The practical aspects of trying to keep these pharmaceutical plants separate from the regular food plants is an insurmountable problem," she says. "It just can't be done. It can't be done because of the fallibility of human beings. It can't be done because you can't control pollen flow. It can't be done because you can't control mother nature that way. And if you can't control mother nature and fallible human beings, we've come to the conclusion that you shouldn't try."

Viewpoint 3

> *"Although I acknowledge the risks, I believe that we can and will incorporate gene technology into the ongoing human adventure."*

Human Genetic Engineering Should Be Allowed

Ronald M. Green

In the following viewpoint, Ronald M. Green argues that despite the lack of public support and the inherent risks, genetic modification of humans holds great promise and should move forward. Green denies that genetic modification will reduce parental love and denies that it will decrease human freedom. He acknowledges that there are risks of a class divide but concludes that the technology can be used for a reduction of inequality and a betterment of humanity. Green is Professor for the Study of Ethics and Human Values at Dartmouth College and author of Babies by Design: The Ethics of Genetic Choice *(Yale University Press, 2007).*

As you read, consider the following questions:

1. According to the author, the National Institutes of Health has initiated a ten-year program to advance what technology?

Ronald M. Green, "Building Baby from the Genes Up," *The Washington Post*, April 13, 2008.

2. Green claims that approximately what percentage of Americans are opposed to human genetic engineering?

3. Green concludes that genomic science can result in many improvements, but he cautions in addressing what challenge along the way?

The two British couples no doubt thought that their appeal for medical help in conceiving a child was entirely reasonable. Over several generations, many female members of their families had died of breast cancer. One or both spouses in each couple had probably inherited the genetic mutations for the disease, and they wanted to use in vitro fertilization and preimplantation genetic diagnosis (PGD) to select only the healthy embryos for implantation. Their goal was to eradicate breast cancer from their family lines once and for all.

The Advancement in Genetic Screening

In the United States, this combination of reproductive and genetic medicine—what one scientist has dubbed "reprogenetics"—remains largely unregulated, but Britain has a formal agency, the Human Fertilisation and Embryology Authority (HFEA), that must approve all requests for PGD. In July 2007, after considerable deliberation, the HFEA approved the procedure for both families. The concern was not about the use of PGD to avoid genetic disease, since embryo screening for serious disorders is commonplace now on both sides of the Atlantic. What troubled the HFEA was the fact that an embryo carrying the cancer mutation could go on to live for 40 or 50 years before ever developing cancer, and there was a chance it might never develop. Did this warrant selecting and discarding embryos? To its critics, the HFEA, in approving this request, crossed a bright line separating legitimate medical genetics from the quest for "the perfect baby."

Like it or not, that decision is a sign of things to come—and not necessarily a bad sign. Since the completion of the

Human Genome Project in 2003, our understanding of the genetic bases of human disease and non-disease traits has been growing almost exponentially. The National Institutes of Health has initiated a quest for the "$1,000 genome," a 10-year program to develop machines that could identify all the genetic letters in anyone's genome at low cost (it took more than $3 billion to sequence the first human genome). With this technology, which some believe may be just four or five years away, we could not only scan an individual's—or embryo's—genome, we could also rapidly compare thousands of people and pinpoint those DNA sequences or combinations that underlie the variations that contribute to our biological differences.

With knowledge comes power. If we understand the genetic causes of obesity, for example, we can intervene by means of embryo selection to produce a child with a reduced genetic likelihood of getting fat. Eventually, without discarding embryos at all, we could use gene-targeting techniques to tweak fetal DNA sequences. No child would have to face a lifetime of dieting or experience the health and cosmetic problems associated with obesity. The same is true for cognitive problems such as dyslexia. Geneticists have already identified some of the mutations that contribute to this disorder. Why should a child struggle with reading difficulties when we could alter the genes responsible for the problem?

The Fears About Genetic Manipulation

Many people are horrified at the thought of such uses of genetics, seeing echoes of the 1997 science fiction film *Gattaca*, which depicted a world where parents choose their children's traits. Human weakness has been eliminated through genetic engineering, and the few parents who opt for a "natural" conception run the risk of producing offspring—"invalids" or "degenerates"—who become members of a despised underclass. *Gattaca*'s world is clean and efficient, but its eugenic obsessions have all but extinguished human love and compassion.

These fears aren't limited to fiction. Over the past few years, many bioethicists have spoken out against genetic manipulations. The critics tend to voice at least four major concerns. First, they worry about the effect of genetic selection on parenting. Will our ability to choose our children's biological inheritance lead parents to replace unconditional love with a consumerist mentality that seeks perfection?

Second, they ask whether gene manipulations will diminish our freedom by making us creatures of our genes or our parents' whims. In his book *Enough*, the techno critic Bill McKibben asks: If I am a world-class runner, but my parents inserted the "Sweatworks2010 GenePack" in my genome, can I really feel pride in my accomplishments? Worse, if I refuse to use my costly genetic endowments, will I face relentless pressure to live up to my parents' expectations?

Third, many critics fear that reproductive genetics will widen our social divisions as the affluent "buy" more competitive abilities for their offspring. Will we eventually see "speciation," the emergence of two or more human populations so different that they no longer even breed with one another? Will we recreate the horrors of eugenics that led, in Europe, Asia and the United States, to the sterilization of tens of thousands of people declared to be "unfit" and that in Nazi Germany paved the way for the Holocaust?

Finally, some worry about the religious implications of this technology. Does it amount to a forbidden and prideful "playing God"?

Doubts About the Critics' Concerns

To many, the answers to these questions are clear. Not long ago, when I asked a large class at Dartmouth medical school whether they thought that we should move in the direction of

The Worry About Parental Love

Along with many other opponents of enhancement technologies, Peter Lawler darkly speculates in *Stuck with Virtue* that enhanced children will be less loved than those produced the old-fashioned way: "A world in which children are manufactured and sex and procreation are totally disconnected would surely be one without much love, one where one manufactured being would have little natural or real connection to other manufactured beings."

But Lawler and his *confrères* [colleagues] need not speculate on what happens to parental love in such cases, for we have actual data. As physician Sally Satel notes in the journal *Policy Review*, "For all the deference that conservative bioethics pays to the implicit wisdom of the ages, it rarely mines the recent past for lessons. Instead of concentrating on the ancients, why not also study the history of in vitro fertilization [IVF], paid egg donation, and surrogate motherhood to learn about cultural resistance and adaptation to such practices?" Indeed. Fears about waning parental love and loosening generational ties were expressed by many bioethicists when in vitro fertilization began to be used in the 1970s and 1980s. Forty years later, the evidence is that their worries were overblown. A recent study in the journal *Human Reproduction* finds that IVF children and their parents are as well adjusted as those born in the conventional way. There are no good reasons to doubt that this will not be the case for enhanced children in the future as well.

Ronald Bailey,
"The Case for Enhancing People,"
New Atlantis, *Summer 2011.*

human genetic engineering, more than 80 percent said no. This squares with public opinion polls that show a similar degree of opposition. Nevertheless, "babies by design" are probably in our future—but I think that the critics' concerns may be less troublesome than they first appear.

Will critical scrutiny replace parental love? Not likely. Even today, parents who hope for a healthy child but have one born with disabilities tend to love that child ferociously. The very intensity of parental love is the best protection against its erosion by genetic technologies. Will a child somehow feel less free because parents have helped select his or her traits? The fact is that a child is already remarkably influenced by the genes she inherits. The difference is that we haven't taken control of the process. Yet.

Knowing more about our genes may actually increase our freedom by helping us understand the biological obstacles—and opportunities—we have to work with. Take the case of Tiger Woods. His father, Earl, is said to have handed him a golf club when he was still in the playpen. Earl probably also gave Tiger the genes for some of the traits that help make him a champion golfer. Genes and upbringing worked together to inspire excellence. Does Tiger feel less free because of his inherited abilities? Did he feel pressured by his parents? I doubt it. Of course, his story could have gone the other way, with overbearing parents forcing a child into their mold. But the problem in that case wouldn't be genetics, but bad parenting.

Moving Forward Despite the Risks

Granted, the social effects of reproductive genetics are worrisome. The risks of producing a "genobility," genetic overlords ruling a vast genetic underclass, are real. But genetics could also become a tool for reducing the class divide. Will we see the day when perhaps all youngsters are genetically vaccinated against dyslexia? And how might this contribute to everyone's social betterment?

As for the question of intruding on God's domain, the answer is less clear than the critics believe. The use of genetic medicine to cure or prevent disease is widely accepted by religious traditions, even those that oppose discarding embryos. Speaking in 1982 at the Pontifical Academy of Sciences, Pope John Paul II observed that modern biological research "can ameliorate the condition of those who are affected by chromosomal diseases," and he lauded this as helping to cure "the smallest and weakest of human beings . . . during their intrauterine life or in the period immediately after birth." For Catholicism and some other traditions, it is one thing to cure disease, but another to create children who are faster runners, longer-lived or smarter.

But why should we think that the human genome is a once-and-for-all-finished, untamperable product? All of the biblically derived faiths permit human beings to improve on nature using technology, from agriculture to aviation. Why not improve our genome? I have no doubt that most people considering these questions for the first time are certain that human genetic improvement is a bad idea, but I'd like to shake up that certainty.

Genomic science is racing toward a future in which foreseeable improvements include reduced susceptibility to a host of diseases, increased life span, better cognitive functioning and maybe even cosmetic enhancements such as whiter, straighter teeth. Yes, genetic orthodontics may be in our future. The challenge is to see that we don't also unleash the demons of discrimination and oppression. Although I acknowledge the risks, I believe that we can and will incorporate gene technology into the ongoing human adventure.

Viewpoint 4

> *"As the American writer Bill McKibben has said, while the greatest macro-scale environmental challenge is global warming, the greatest micro-scale environmental challenge is genetic engineering."*

We Must Stop Trying to Engineer Nature

Mark Lynas

In the following viewpoint, Mark Lynas argues that genetic engineering may have some good applications, but it also has some bad applications, and problems arise when society is not adequately prepared to regulate or stop scientific research that has potential for harm. He argues that scientists may promote their own agendas in a way that obscures the ethical issues raised by their work. However, human biotechnology gives power over the future of the human species to scientists, corporations, and governments. According to Lynas, this raises serious concerns about the stability of the biological and social foundations of humanity. Lynas is an environmental activist and a climate change specialist. He is the author of High Tide: News from a Warming World *and* Six Degrees: Our Future on a Hotter Planet.

As you read, consider the following questions:

1. What is an example of a good use and an example of a bad use of reproductive technology, according to the author?
2. What argument do scientists use to promote their opinions and obscure ethical issues about genetic engineering, according to the author?
3. What is Dr. Richard Hayes reported to have said about the ability to manipulate human nature?

How suffering may be bad but the alternative could prove to be far, far worse.

Any bereaved parent can tell you that nothing compares with the pain of losing a child. When my sister-in-law and her husband lost their first child—a baby just four months old—to cystic fibrosis, their world literally collapsed. Tests soon confirmed that both parents were carriers of the CF gene, so any future baby would have a worrying one-in-four chance of inheriting the condition. But reproductive technology offered a solution: embryos were created through in vitro fertilisation and cells were screened for the disease, after which only CF-free embryos were implanted. The process worked, and Sue and Chris now have two happy and healthy children.

This story illustrates how advances in medical knowledge can be of great benefit. But now consider another true story, this time from Texas in the United States, where the world's first human embryo bank was launched last year. For a mere £5,000, prospective parents can buy embryos via mail order, their genetic parents pre-specified for blond hair and blue eyes if necessary. The Abraham Centre of Life even boasts that all its sperm donors have doctorate degrees. Its director, Jennalee Ryan, is untroubled by the ethical issues raised by her company. "We are helping couples and putting good genes back into the universe," she boasts.

What these two stories show is that identical technologies—in this case, in reproductive medicine—can have good and bad applications. There is nothing new in this: the radiotherapy that cures cancer also allows us to have the atom bomb. Problems arise when society at large has insufficient expertise or foreknowledge to regulate, and if necessary stymie, new areas of scientific research as they come into being. The situation is made worse when the scientists in question aggressively push their opinions in the press, and seek actively to obscure the ethical issues that their work is raising in order to head off any potentially restrictive legislation.

A recent example is a group of senior scientists who wrote a furious letter to the *Times* in January, attacking government proposals to outlaw the creation of human-animal hybrid embryos on the grounds that this will hold up research into treatments for Alzheimer's and other neuro-degenerative diseases. As so often with genetics research, the potential to treat human diseases is wielded as an ethical cover to trump any legitimate wider concerns. Implanting human-cell nuclei in cow eggs may or may not eventually help people with Alzheimer's, but the implications of this technology are highly disturbing, even at this early stage.

Indeed, the whole science of genetics raises serious concerns about the future direction of human civilisation. As the American writer Bill McKibben has said, while the greatest macro-scale environmental challenge is global warming, the greatest micro-scale environmental challenge is genetic engineering. With each leap in technical understanding, scientists—and the corporations and governments that employ them—accumulate ever greater power, intentionally or unintentionally, over the future of the human species. Although crude eugenics and racial cleansing are generally held to have died out with the Nazis, the commodification of human reproduction could lead us blindly down the same eventual path.

Familiar moral lenses may offer little guidance. Stem cell research and the cloning of embryos are most vociferously opposed by the pro-life and religious lobbies, but the purported rights of embryos are far from being the most important ethical issues they raise. The wider implications of human biotechnology are discussed in a thoughtful article in the March/April issue of *World Watch* magazine. As Dr Richard Hayes, director of the Center for Genetics and Society in California, puts it: "The ability to manipulate human nature destabilises both the biological and social foundations of the human world."

As an environmentalist, I profoundly oppose these trends. Even allowing for their purported benefits—in the case of Alzheimer's, for example, or cystic fibrosis—the cure may end up being worse than the disease, as we find a society with increasing technological power over human life itself increasingly abusing what it means to be free and human. I want to see a society in which humanity stops trying to control nature, and learns to live within its physical, biological and spiritual boundaries. That does mean facing certain difficult realities, such as the fact that all of us will die one day. But nature shows us that death brings new life, and that this must be consolation enough. Suffering may be bad, but the alternative may prove to be far, far worse.

VIEWPOINT 5

> *"The majority of Americans—from across the political spectrum, and of all backgrounds and beliefs—have come to a consensus that we should pursue this research."*

Stem Cell Research Should Be Allowed, but Not Reproductive Cloning

Barack Obama

In the following viewpoint, Barack Obama defends his decision to lift the ban on federal funding for stem cell research, arguing that the majority of Americans support such research. Obama contends that although research using stem cells should be done in pursuit of cures for health conditions, he claims that the research guidelines will be strict and will not allow cloning for human reproduction. He concludes that the research should be pursued with integrity, free of political manipulation. Obama is the forty-fourth president of the United States.

As you read, consider the following questions:

1. Name at least three of the health conditions that Obama claims scientists believe may have treatment or cures from stem cells.

Barack Obama, "Remarks of President Barack Obama—As Prepared for Delivery Signing of Stem Cell Executive Order and Scientific Integrity Presidential Memorandum," Office of the Press Secretary, White House, March 9, 2009.

2. The author claims that the perils of stem cell research can be avoided with what?
3. What two advocates of stem cell research does Obama name as being owed a debt of gratitude for bringing attention to the cause?

Today [March 9, 2009], with the executive order I am about to sign, we will bring the change that so many scientists and researchers; doctors and innovators; patients and loved ones have hoped for, and fought for, these past eight years: We will lift the ban on federal funding for promising embryonic stem cell research. We will vigorously support scientists who pursue this research. And we will aim for America to lead the world in the discoveries it one day may yield.

The Promise of Stem Cell Research

At this moment, the full promise of stem cell research remains unknown, and it should not be overstated. But scientists believe these tiny cells may have the potential to help us understand, and possibly cure, some of our most devastating diseases and conditions. To regenerate a severed spinal cord and lift someone from a wheelchair. To spur insulin production and spare a child from a lifetime of needles. To treat Parkinson's [disease], cancer, heart disease and others that affect millions of Americans and the people who love them.

But that potential will not reveal itself on its own. Medical miracles do not happen simply by accident. They result from painstaking and costly research—from years of lonely trial and error, much of which never bears fruit—and from a government willing to support that work. From lifesaving vaccines, to pioneering cancer treatments, to the sequencing of the human genome—that is the story of scientific progress in America. When government fails to make these investments, opportunities are missed. Promising avenues go unexplored. Some of our best scientists leave for other countries that will sponsor their work. And those countries may surge ahead of ours in the advances that transform our lives.

But in recent years, when it comes to stem cell research, rather than furthering discovery, our government has forced what I believe is a false choice between sound science and moral values. In this case, I believe the two are not inconsistent. As a person of faith, I believe we are called to care for each other and work to ease human suffering. I believe we have been given the capacity and will to pursue this research—and the humanity and conscience to do so responsibly.

A Delicate Balance

It is a difficult and delicate balance. Many thoughtful and decent people are conflicted about, or strongly oppose, this research. I understand their concerns, and we must respect their point of view.

But after much discussion, debate, and reflection, the proper course has become clear. The majority of Americans—from across the political spectrum, and of all backgrounds and beliefs—have come to a consensus that we should pursue this research. That the potential it offers is great, and with proper guidelines and strict oversight, the perils can be avoided.

That is a conclusion with which I agree. That is why I am signing this executive order, and why I hope Congress will act on a bipartisan basis to provide further support for this research. We are joined today by many leaders who have reached across the aisle to champion this cause, and I commend them for that work.

Ultimately, I cannot guarantee that we will find the treatments and cures we seek. No president can promise that. But I can promise that we will seek them—actively, responsibly, and with the urgency required to make up for lost ground. Not just by opening up this new frontier of research today, but by

Americans' Views on Therapeutic Cloning

Do you favor or oppose using human cloning technology IF it is used ONLY to help medical research develop new treatments for disease—do you strongly favor, somewhat favor, somewhat oppose, or strongly oppose this?

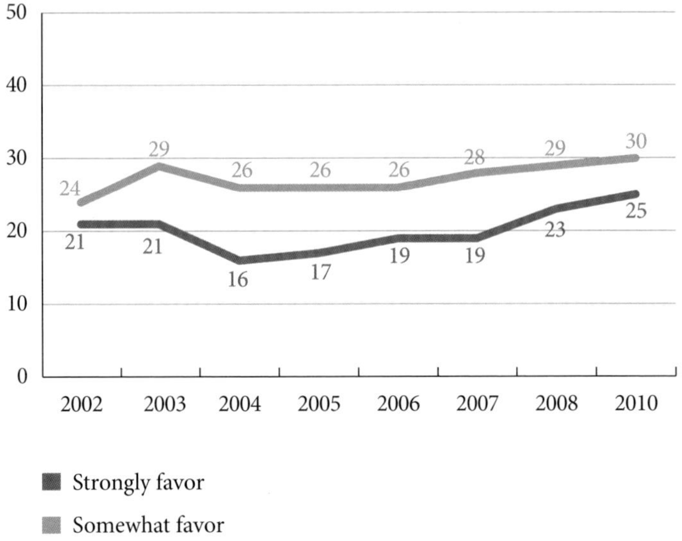

TAKEN FROM: VCU Life Sciences Survey 2010, May 12–18, 2010. www.vcu.edu.

supporting promising research of all kinds, including groundbreaking work to convert ordinary human cells into ones that resemble embryonic stem cells.

I can also promise that we will never undertake this research lightly. We will support it only when it is both scientifically worthy and responsibly conducted. We will develop strict guidelines, which we will rigorously enforce, because we cannot ever tolerate misuse or abuse. And we will ensure that our government never opens the door to the use of cloning for human reproduction. It is dangerous, profoundly wrong, and has no place in our society, or any society.

A Commitment to Scientific Integrity

This order is an important step in advancing the cause of science in America. But let's be clear: Promoting science isn't just about providing resources—it is also about protecting free and open inquiry. It is about letting scientists like those here today do their jobs, free from manipulation or coercion, and listening to what they tell us, even when it's inconvenient—especially when it's inconvenient. It is about ensuring that scientific data is never distorted or concealed to serve a political agenda—and that we make scientific decisions based on facts, not ideology.

By doing this, we will ensure America's continued global leadership in scientific discoveries and technological breakthroughs. That is essential not only for our economic prosperity, but for the progress of all humanity.

That is why today, I am also signing a presidential memorandum directing the head of the White House Office of Science and Technology Policy to develop a strategy for restoring scientific integrity to government decision making. To ensure that in this new administration, we base our public policies on the soundest science; that we appoint scientific advisors based on their credentials and experience, not their politics or ideology; and that we are open and honest with the American people about the science behind our decisions. That is how we will harness the power of science to achieve our goals—to preserve our environment and protect our national security; to create the jobs of the future; and live longer, healthier lives.

The Ongoing Work of Science

As we restore our commitment to science, and resume funding for promising stem cell research, we owe a debt of gratitude to so many tireless advocates, some of whom are with us today, many of whom are not. Today, we honor all those whose names we don't know, who organized, and raised awareness, and kept on fighting—even when it was too late for them, or for the people they love. And we honor those we know, who used their influence to help others and bring attention to this cause—people like [quadriplegic actor] Christopher and Dana Reeve, who we wish could be here to see this moment.

One of Christopher's friends recalled that he hung a sign on the wall of the exercise room where he did his grueling regimen of physical therapy. It read: "For everyone who thought I couldn't do it. For everyone who thought I shouldn't do it. For everyone who said, 'It's impossible.' See you at the finish line."

Christopher once told a reporter who was interviewing him: "If you came back here in ten years, I expect that I'd walk to the door to greet you."

Christopher did not get that chance. But if we pursue this research, maybe one day—maybe not in our lifetime, or even in our children's lifetime—but maybe one day, others like him might.

There is no finish line in the work of science. The race is always with us—the urgent work of giving substance to hope and answering those many bedside prayers, of seeking a day when words like "terminal" and "incurable" are finally retired from our vocabulary.

Today, using every resource at our disposal, with renewed determination to lead the world in the discoveries of this new century, we rededicate ourselves to this work.

VIEWPOINT 6

> *"The door to human cloning should not only be shut, it should be slammed shut and locked forever."*

Ignored Implications

Ken Blackwell

In the following viewpoint, Ken Blackwell argues that there are serious moral problems with embryonic stem cell research. Blackwell contends that the law should protect life by not allowing embryonic stem cells to be harvested since the process requires the destruction of human embryos. Additionally, Blackwell claims that any human cloning, whether for use in therapeutic stem cell treatment or reproduction, should not be allowed because it entails the growing of human beings to be used in treatment or research. Blackwell is a senior fellow with the Family Research Council.

As you read, consider the following questions:

1. For what reason does Blackwell suggest that stem cell research may be utterly unnecessary?
2. Why were no medical advances missed during the years there was a ban on stem cell research, according to the author?

3. According to Blackwell, what two past presidents opposed human cloning?

By signing an executive order on embryonic stem cell research, President Obama opened a door that should forever be slammed shut.

President Obama recently made the wrong move by incurring additional federal debt for research on human embryos and—contrary to what many have said in the media—opening the door to human cloning. He has drawn a sharp distinction between the political parties, and announced that he will cross the Rubicon on an issue with frightening implications for America's future.

Stem cells are generated in various ways. For a number of years, many scientists were particularly interested in cells derived from fertilized human embryos that are only a few days old. The cells generated by these embryos—called undifferentiated pluripotent stem cells—are thought by some to be capable of all sorts of medical treatments.

The moral problem with obtaining them is this: It destroys the young human embryo in the process.

From the outset, it's important to recognize the facts, because both politicians and many in the media have grossly distorted this issue.

First, this research may be utterly unnecessary. Americans don't need to navigate the ethical dilemmas of embryonic stem cell research if the results gained from this research could be safely derived from other sources. Although many in the media chose to ignore it, scientists have discovered a method whereby adult skin cells can be modified in a way that appears to give them all the properties of embryonic stem cells. Those on the political left ignored this breakthrough, although it received notice in nonconservative journals such as *Science, Cell, Wired*, and *National Geographic*.

Second, former president Bush was the first president to provide federal funding for embryonic stem cell research. But

Cloning Is Cloning

All cloning is reproductive cloning because, if successful, it always reproduces another human being. There are not different types of cloning—cloning is cloning; the only question that arises is what one intends to do with the newly created cloned embryo—implant him or her in a womb to try for a live birth, or destroy him or her for research purposes.

Gene Tarne, "Cloning Is Cloning Is Cloning . . . ," American Thinker, *May 1, 2011.*

he provided that funding only to the cell lines that currently existed, from embryos that had already been destroyed. Bush explained that the life-or-death decision was already off the table for those cell lines, providing funding for research on them but refusing to fund future destruction of human embryos.

This policy, however, did nothing to restrict private research on human embryos. Under current law, stem cell research went on for years at private research institutions, funded by private dollars. Even if embryonic stem cells were necessary for certain research, no supposed medical advances were missed because this private-sector research continued full throttle.

From a moral perspective, if the law must err, it should err on the side of protecting life. In one of the flimsiest dodges of the election season, Barack Obama, during a televised forum, ducked a question from the Rev. Rick Warren on abortion by saying that the question of when human life begins is above his pay grade. When you're president of the United States, nothing is above your pay grade if it's a topic where the president makes policy decisions. If President Obama was convinced that destroying fertilized, growing, days-old embryos was not ending human lives, then that would be something to debate. But when he readily says he doesn't know when life begins—leaving open the possibility these brand-new creatures are human beings—then he should err on the side of caution by not funding their annihilation.

This becomes all the more apparent with the recent skin cell breakthrough. If skin cells can harmlessly be used to deliver all the same research as stem cells, then it shocks the conscience that anyone would insist on continuing to destroy human embryos. At the very least, if there is any doubt as to whether these skin cells offer the same promise, then President Obama should wait until the science on the issue is clear.

But it gets worse. When human cloning looked like a near-term possibility in the 1990s, it was President Bill Clinton who first put into law a prohibition against it. President George W. Bush then renewed this ban. Both presidents—of different parties—drew a clear line in the sand that cloning human beings was a moral and ethical line we would never cross as a nation.

Then President Obama arrived. In the same speech where he authorized the new stem cell funding, he announced he would also not allow human cloning for purposes of reproduction. He clearly left the door open to allow cloning for medical research purposes. In a way that was considered unthinkable during every American administration in the past, President Obama refuses to rule out allowing scientists to actually grow human beings in a laboratory, to harvest their body parts, and conduct research for the benefit of other human beings.

And most in the media ignored this disturbing shift in American policy.

No human being should ever be killed to benefit another human being. Such a policy would put America on a path that would lead to terrifying results. The door to human cloning should not only be shut, it should be slammed shut and locked forever.

The American people voted for change. Does anyone believe this is what they had in mind?

Periodical and Internet Sources Bibliography

The following articles have been selected to supplement the diverse views presented in this chapter.

Ronald Bailey	"The Case for Enhancing People," *New Atlantis*, Summer 2011.
Nick Bostrom	"In Defense of Posthuman Dignity," *Bioethics*, vol. 19, no. 3, 2005.
Andy Coghlan	"Here Come the Designer Babies," *New Scientist*, May 12, 2008.
Gregg Easterbrook	"Embrace Human Cloning," *Wired*, October 2009.
Daniel Finkelstein	"Choosing a Deaf Child Is Criminal," *Times* (United Kingdom), March 12, 2008.
Allen Goldberg	"Select a Baby's Health, Not Eye Color," *Los Angeles Times*, February 17, 2009.
Terry Jeffrey	"Obama's Carefully Crafted Cloning Contradiction," Townhall.com, March 11, 2009.
Patrick Lin	"More than Human? The Ethics of Biologically Enhancing Soldiers," *Atlantic*, February 16, 2012.
George Neumayr	"Three Humans and an Embryo," *American Spectator*, April 16, 2010.
William Saletan	"Leave This Child Behind: Sports, Segregation, and Environmental Eugenics," *Slate*, December 1, 2008.
Benjamin Storey	"Liberation Biology, Lost in the Cosmos," *New Atlantis*, Summer 2011.
Gene Tarne	"Cloning Is Cloning Is Cloning . . . ," *American Thinker*, May 1, 2011.

OPPOSING VIEWPOINTS® SERIES

Chapter 2

What Are the Benefits and Risks of Genetic Engineering?

Chapter Preface

The potential benefits of genetic engineering are promising, but as with any new technology, there are concerns about risks. Genetic engineering could allow scientists to replace a missing or defective gene with a working copy of that gene. Assuming that the new gene could function properly, individuals could be cured of numerous diseases. Researchers have made headway in finding single genes that are responsible for diseases such as cystic fibrosis, and progress is being made in finding multiple genes responsible for other diseases such as cancer and AIDS. This kind of gene therapy is still in the experimental stage, and the experiments themselves are controversial because of the risks involved. There is debate about allowing the research to move forward since it inevitably involves the use of willing human subjects. One recent gene-therapy clinical trial illustrates the concern about balancing benefits and risks.

X-linked severe combined immunodeficiency (X-SCID) is an inherited disorder of the immune system that mainly affects boys. Boys born with X-SCID are prone to recurrent bacterial, viral, and fungal infections that cause serious illnesses. Without intervention, the disease often causes death in the first year of life. A gene-therapy trial took place in Paris between 1999 and 2002 in which nine male infants with X-SCID underwent gene therapy in an attempt to cure the condition. The therapy was initially successful in correcting the immune system dysfunction. Later, however, four of those boys developed leukemia and one died. Nonetheless, almost a decade later, seven of the nine boys—three surviving leukemia—had sustained immune reconstitution from the therapy and were living normal lives. Other trials for X-SCID have yielded similar results, where the treatment is successful in correcting the immune dysfunction for the majority of participants but carries the risk of leukemia and death.

When gene therapy is used for life-threatening diseases, the fact that it may itself cause a life-threatening disease must be weighed against the possible benefit of full recovery. When no other treatment is available for a fatal illness, a strong argument can be made that the possibility of recovery outweighs the risk of possible death. Furthermore, by allowing the clinical trials, scientists can learn more about the risks of certain gene therapies and work to reduce those risks with new procedures. In fact, after the Paris clinical trial, researchers modified the treatment for X-SCID in the hopes that the risk of leukemia would be lessened. Of course, when gene therapy is used for diseases that are not life threatening but still have the risk of death, the argument for its use is not as strong. In all cases of genetic engineering technology, this kind of balancing of the benefits and risks can help to inform the wisdom of moving forward with its use.

Viewpoint 1

> *"If [genetically modified] foods on the market cause common diseases, mild symptoms, or have long-term impacts, we may never know. There's no monitoring."*

Genetically Modified Foods Could Pose Numerous Health Risks

Institute for Responsible Technology

In the following viewpoint, the Institute for Responsible Technology argues that there is no reason to believe genetically modified (GM) food is safe, but there are several reasons to believe that GM food poses health risks to humans. The institute claims that several animal studies show health problems resulting from consumption of GM food, raising serious questions about the safety for humans. The Institute for Responsible Technology is an organization that aims to educate policy makers and the public about genetically modified (GM) foods and crops.

As you read, consider the following questions:

1. According to the author, since what year have genetically modified plants had genes from bacteria and viruses forced into their DNA?

"Doctors' Health Warning: Avoid Genetically Modified Foods," Institute for Responsible Technology, 2011, pp. 1–7.

2. What are the six major genetically modified crops, according to the author?
3. The author claims that farmers in Europe and Asia reported deaths of what animals from eating genetically modified corn?

The American Academy of Environmental Medicine (AAEM) urges physicians to advise all patients to avoid genetically modified (GM) food.

They state, "Several animal studies indicate serious health risks associated with GM food." These include:

- Infertility
- Immune problems
- Accelerated aging
- Faulty insulin regulation
- Changes in major organs and the gastrointestinal system.

Since 1996, GM plants such as soybeans and corn have genes from bacteria and viruses forced into their DNA. Most Americans don't realize that they eat GM ingredients in most processed foods.

A Question of Safety

The Food and Drug Administration [FDA] policy on genetically modified organisms (GMOs), released in 1992, falsely claims that the agency had no information showing that GM foods are substantially different. Thousands of secret memos later made public by a lawsuit reveal just the opposite. FDA scientists repeatedly warned of possible allergies, toxins, new diseases, and nutritional problems; they urged long-term safety studies. But the FDA official in charge of policy was Michael Taylor, Monsanto's former attorney, later their vice president, and now the US food safety czar.

The FDA ignored their scientists, and doesn't require a single safety test. Instead, companies such as Monsanto, which have been found guilty of hiding toxic effects of their other products, get to decide if their GMOs are safe for us to eat. And the superficial studies they do conduct are widely criticized as rigged to avoid finding problems.

Gene insertion into plants is done by shooting cells with a "gene gun" or using bacteria to infect the cells. Then the cells are cloned into plants. These laboratory techniques are imprecise and bear no resemblance to natural breeding. The technology is based on outdated scientific assumptions and can lead to massive collateral damage in the plant. The DNA of GMOs, for example, can have hundreds or thousands of mutations, and the activity of up to 5% of their natural genes can be significantly changed. Even the inserted gene can be damaged or rearranged, creating proteins that trigger allergies or promote disease.

GM Foods on the Market

The six major GMO crops are soy, corn, canola, cotton, sugar beets, and alfalfa. Each has added bacterial genes, allowing plants to survive an otherwise deadly dose of weed killer such as Roundup. Farmers use considerably more herbicide on these crops, causing higher herbicide residues in our food.

The second most popular trait is a built-in pesticide, found in GM corn and cotton. An inserted gene from soil bacteria called Bt (*Bacillus thuringiensis*) secretes the insect-killing Bt toxin in every cell.

The other GM crops are Hawaiian papaya and a small amount of zucchini and yellow crookneck squash, which are engineered to resist a plant virus.

GMOs and Allergic Reactions

- Soy allergies skyrocketed by 50% in the UK [United Kingdom], soon after GM soy was introduced.

Industry Is in Charge of Safety

Ironically, policy makers around the world gain confidence in the safety of GM [genetically modified] crops because they wrongly assume that the US FDA [Food and Drug Administration] has approved them based on extensive tests, and approvals everywhere rely on the developers to do safety studies on their own crops. Research does not need to be published and most is kept secret under the guise of "confidential business information." Very little data is available for public scrutiny. In 2003, for example, researchers reviewed published, peer-reviewed animal feeding studies that qualified as safety assessments. There were ten. The correlation between the findings and the funding was telling. Five studies "performed more or less in collaboration with private companies" reported no adverse effects. In the three independent studies, "adverse effects were reported." The authors said, "It is remarkable that these effects have all been observed after feeding for only 10–14 days."

Jeffrey M. Smith,
Genetic Roulette: The Documented
Health Risks of Genetically Engineered Foods.
White River Junction, VT: Chelsea Green, 2007, p. 2.

- Cooked GM soy contains as much as 7 times the amount of a known soy allergen.
- GM corn contains an allergen not found in natural varieties.
- GM soy also has an allergen not found in wild soy, and some people react in a skin prick allergy test to the GM variety, but not the wild type.

Natural Bt bacteria has been used in spray form by farmers for years, although it biodegrades quickly. The Bt in GM crops is designed to be more toxic than the natural spray, is thousands of times more concentrated, and doesn't biodegrade.

Hundreds of people exposed to natural Bt spray had allergic symptoms, and mice fed natural Bt toxin had damaged intestines and powerful immune responses. Now mice and rats fed Bt corn show immune responses, and people exposed to Bt cotton are getting the allergic reactions.

A study in Canada found Bt toxin and herbicide residues from GM crops in the blood of women and fetuses.

No tests can guarantee that a GMO will not cause allergies. Although the World Health Organization recommends a screening protocol, the GM soy, corn, and papaya in our food supply fail those tests—because their GM proteins have properties of known allergens.

The Effects of GMOs on Animals

- GM soy drastically reduces digestive enzymes in mice. If it also impairs your digestion, you may become sensitive and allergic to a variety of foods.
- Mice fed Bt toxin started having immune reactions to formerly harmless foods.
- Mice fed experimental GM peas also started reacting to a range of other foods. (The peas had already passed the allergy tests normally done before a GMO gets on the market. Only this advanced test, which is never used on the GMOs we eat, revealed that the peas might actually be deadly.)
- More than half the babies of mother rats fed GM soy died within three weeks.
- Rodents fed GM soy had changes in their ovaries, uterus, or testicles, including altered young sperm cells.

- The DNA of mouse embryos functioned differently when the parents ate GM soy.
- Mice fed GM corn had fertility problems and smaller babies.
- By the third generation, most hamsters fed GM soy were unable to have babies and suffered high infant mortality; some had hair growing in their mouths.
- Farmers in Europe and Asia say that cows, water buffaloes, chickens, and horses died from eating Bt corn varieties.
- About two dozen US farmers report that Bt corn varieties caused widespread sterility in pigs or cows.
- Filipinos in at least five villages fell sick when a nearby Bt corn variety was pollinating.

Other Dangers of GMOs

The only published human feeding experiment on GMOs revealed that the genetic material inserted into GM soy transfers into bacteria living inside our intestines and continues to function. This means that long after we stop eating GM foods, we may still have their GM proteins produced continuously inside us.

- If the antibiotic gene inserted into most GM crops were to transfer, it could create super diseases resistant to antibiotics.
- If the gene that creates Bt toxin in GM corn were to transfer, it might turn our intestinal bacteria into living pesticide factories.
- Animal studies show that DNA in food can travel into organs throughout the body, even into the fetus.

In the 1980s, a contaminated brand of a food supplement called L-tryptophan killed about 100 Americans and caused sickness and disability in another 5,000–10,000 people. The source of contaminants was almost certainly the genetic engineering process used in its production. The disease was only identified because the symptoms had three simultaneous characteristics: they were unique, acute, and fast acting. If GM foods on the market cause common diseases, mild symptoms, or have long-term impacts, we may never know. There's no monitoring and hardly any long-term animal studies. So we can't say for sure if GMOs contribute to the recent rise in chronic illness, food allergies, reproductive and digestive problems, autism, and other disorders. But medical organizations like the AAEM say we shouldn't keep eating GMOs while waiting for more studies.

Viewpoint 2

"Responding to the bleating of activists, policy makers have subjected the testing and commercialization of genetically engineered crops to unscientific and draconian regulations, with dire consequences."

Genetically Modified Foods Have Numerous Benefits and No Known Risks

Henry I. Miller

In the following viewpoint, Henry I. Miller argues that capitulation by food companies to activists in ceasing use of genetically engineered ingredients is dangerous and not supported by science. Miller contends that genetic engineering actually makes food safer by reducing such dangerous contaminants as fungus and mold. He concludes that making policy based on irrational technophobia is dangerous to consumers and food producers. Miller is a physician and molecular biologist, a fellow at Stanford University's Hoover Institution, and coauthor of The Frankenfood Myth: How Protest and Politics Threaten the Biotech Revolution.

As you read, consider the following questions:

1. According to the author, which six food manufacturers have eliminated genetically engineered ingredients as a result of pressure from activists?
2. Miller claims that research shows that the level of fumonisin in genetically modified corn is lowered by what percentage compared to conventional corn?
3. Name at least two demonstrated, significant benefits of genetically engineered foods listed by the author.

During the late 1990s, a singular phenomenon appeared in countries around the world. One after another, food and beverage companies capitulated to activists opposed to a promising new technology: the genetic engineering of plants to produce ingredients. They are still capitulating to this day [in 2012].

The Rise of Technophobia

The Japanese brewer Kirin and the Danish brewer Carlsberg eliminated genetically engineered ingredients from their beers. In the United States, the fast-food giant McDonald's banned them from its menu; food manufacturers Heinz and Gerber (then a division of Switzerland-based Novartis) dropped them from their baby-food lines; and Frito-Lay demanded that its growers stop planting corn engineered to contain a bacterial protein that confers resistance to insect predation.

These measures were rationalized in various ways, but the reality is that by yielding to the demands of a minuscule number of disingenuous activists, the companies opted to offer less safe products to consumers, thereby exposing themselves to legal jeopardy.

Every year, innumerable packaged-food products worldwide are withheld or recalled from the market due to the presence of "all natural" contaminants like insect parts, toxic molds, bacteria, and viruses. Because farming takes place outdoors and in dirt, such contamination is a fact of life. Over the centuries, the main culprit in mass food poisoning often has been contamination of unprocessed crops by fungal toxins—a risk that is exacerbated when insects attack food crops, opening wounds that allow fungi (molds) to get a foothold.

The Danger of Fungal Toxins

For example, fumonisin and some other fungal toxins are highly toxic, causing esophageal cancer in humans and fatal diseases in livestock that eat infected corn. Fumonisin also interferes with the cellular uptake of folic acid, a vitamin that reduces the risk of neural tube defects in developing fetuses, and thus can cause folic acid deficiency—and defects such as spina bifida—even when one's diet contains what otherwise would be sufficient amounts of the vitamin.

Many regulatory agencies have therefore established recommended maximum fumonisin levels permitted in food and feed products made from corn. The conventional way to meet those standards and prevent the consumption of fungal toxins is simply to test unprocessed and processed grains and discard those found to be contaminated—an approach that is both wasteful and failure prone.

But modern technology—specifically, the genetic engineering of plants using recombinant DNA technology (also known as food biotechnology or genetic modification)—offers a way to prevent the problem. Contrary to the claims of food-biotech critics, who insist that genetically modified crops pose risks (none of which has actually occurred) of new allergens or toxins in the food supply, such products offer the food industry a proven and practical means of tackling the fungal contamination at its source.

The Benefits of Genetic Engineering

An excellent example is corn that is crafted by splicing into commercial varieties a gene (or genes) from a harmless bacte-

The Activists' Strategy

The activists' strategy is reminiscent of the old courtroom dictum: When the facts are on your side, pound the facts; when the facts are against you, pound the table. Because there is no scientific evidence to support allegations about negative effects of genetic engineering, they are pounding the table, resorting to scare tactics and wholly unfounded assertions. Nowhere in the peer-reviewed studies or monitoring programs of the past 30 years is there persuasive evidence of health or environmental problems stemming from genetically engineered seeds or crops. Quite the opposite: The technology used to produce these seeds is a paragon of agricultural progress and benefit to the natural environment.

Gregory Conko and Henry I. Miller,
"The Rush to Condemn Genetically Modified Crops,"
Policy Review, *no. 165, February/March 2011.*

rium. The bacterial genes express proteins that are toxic to corn-boring insects, but that are harmless to birds, fish, and mammals, including humans. As the modified corn fends off insect pests, it also reduces the levels of the mold *Fusarium*, thereby reducing the levels of fumonisin.

Indeed, researchers at Iowa State University and the US Department of Agriculture have found that the level of fumonisin in the modified corn is reduced by as much as 80% compared to conventional corn. Similarly, an Italian study of weaned piglets that were fed either conventional corn or the same variety modified to synthesize a bacterial protein that confers resistance to insect predation found that the modified variety contained lower levels of fumonisin. More importantly, the piglets that consumed the modified corn achieved a greater final weight, a measure of overall health, despite no difference in feed intake between the two groups.

Given the health benefits—to say nothing of the often higher and more reliable yields—governments should introduce incentives aimed at increasing use of such genetically engineered grains and other crops. In addition, one would expect public health advocates to demand that such improved varieties be cultivated and used for food, not unlike requirements that drinking water be chlorinated and fluoridated. And food producers that are committed to offering the safest and best products to their customers should be competing to get genetically engineered products into the marketplace.

Alas, none of this has come to pass. Activists continue to mount vocal and tenacious opposition to genetically engineered foods, despite almost 20 years of demonstrated, significant benefits, including reduced use of chemical pesticides (and thus less chemical runoff into waterways), greater use of farming practices that prevent soil erosion, higher profits for farmers, and less fungal contamination.

Dangerous Public Policy

Responding to the bleating of activists, policy makers have subjected the testing and commercialization of genetically engineered crops to unscientific and draconian regulations, with dire consequences. A groundbreaking study of the political economy of agricultural biotechnology [by Gregory D. Graff, Gal Hochman, and David Zilberman] concluded that overregulation causes "delays in the global diffusion of proven technologies, resulting in a lower rate of growth in the global food supply and higher food prices." Current policies also create "disincentives for investing in further research and development, resulting in a slowdown in innovation of second-generation technologies anticipated to introduce broad consumer and environmental benefits."

Everyone involved in food production and consumption has suffered: consumers (especially in developing countries) have been subjected to avoidable health risks, and food producers have placed themselves in legal jeopardy for selling products known to have "design defects."

Public policy that discriminates against and discourages vital innovations in food production is not policy that has the public's interest at heart.

VIEWPOINT 3

"While naysayers declare genetic modification to be a new and evil practice . . . [researcher Pam Ronald] says the line between 'genetically engineered' and 'traditional' crops really exists only in the media and politics."

Genetically Modified Crops Can Increase Productivity to End World Hunger

Erik Vance

In the following viewpoint, Erik Vance contends that a new revolution is occurring in agricultural research that uses genetic engineering, along with organic farming, to increase food productivity and security. Vance claims that scientists have developed flood-proof rice through genetic transfer that can address the threat of climate change to rice crops in the developing world. He concludes that the debate about good and bad agricultural practices is turning out to be full of false dichotomies. Vance is a science writer.

Erik Vance, "Genetically Modified Conservation," *Conservation Magazine*, vol. 11, no. 3, July/September 2010.

As you read, consider the following questions:

1. Why was the so-called Green Revolution of the mid-twentieth century not so green after all, according to Vance?
2. According to the author, flooding in Southeast Asia currently causes how much monetary damage to rice crops annually?
3. How many Americans are killed by pesticides each year, according to Vance?

In the mid-1940s, [American agronomist] Norman Borlaug started the Green Revolution on a small farm in southern Mexico. His idea was simple. As the human population skyrocketed, he would grow a new kind of wheat with a thicker stem and bigger seed heads, thus increasing its yield and allowing farmers to grow more wheat—and feed more people—per acre.

The results were staggering. Within two decades, Mexico's wheat harvest had swollen sixfold, thanks to crops descended from Borlaug's original modified wheat. Borlaug then turned his talents toward rice in the Philippines, and high-yield crops spread into almost every major food staple. In all, Borlaug's revolution helped feed millions of people in poor and developing countries who would otherwise have starved—an achievement that earned him the 1970 Nobel Peace Prize.

A New Revolution

But the Green Revolution wasn't "green" in the modern sense of the word. In fact, it exacted a huge environmental toll. Its crops require liberal use of fertilizer and pesticides that bleed into the land and sea, poisoning wildlife and creating nitrogen-rich dead zones in the oceans.

Now, with climate change threatening to upend many of the world's crops, a new generation of researchers is poised to correct some of the original revolution's flaws and rethink agriculture once again. One of its newest spokespersons is Pam Ronald, a University of California-Davis researcher who sees a future dominated not by Monsanto-like corporations but by small partnerships between farmers and scientists.

By combining genetically modified crops with organic farming and other eco-friendly practices, Ronald believes, we can create a system that slashes pesticide use, insulates crops against floods and drought, and protects the livelihoods of poor farmers in the developing world. To many, the idea of using genetic engineering as a conservation tool is an oxymoron, but the scales may finally be tipping in Ronald's favor.

Her ideas have drawn attention at the highest levels and [have] become a favorite of opinion makers such as Michael Pollan and Bill Gates. What's more, they serve as a stark reminder that genetically modified foods are here—whether we like it or not. Which means that, at a time when we need to reinvent the world's food supply, the critical question may be can we get it right?

A Plant Geneticist

Ronald is an unlikely genetic-engineering advocate. Pulling into her driveway, I see that her yard looks like that of any eco-foodie. Her garden—a tangled mix of herbs and native plants—has a happy, New Age feel. Her barn sports a mural that is "Diego Rivera meets Cesar Chavez." And her husband, Raoul Adamchak, is an organic farmer.

But Ronald, a plant geneticist, is also an unabashed supporter of genetically modified (GM) crops. Her recent book on the benefits of bioengineered organic crops, *Tomorrow's Table* (which she cowrote with Adamchak), has started reshaping the way we look at GM foods.

While the GM debate has traditionally been focused on genetically modified corn and other lucrative foodstuffs, Ronald has been doing pioneering work on a crop that is largely ignored: rice. In fact, while companies such as Monsanto pour billions into GM crops, rice research is almost solely the province of publicly funded academics. "The big companies aren't working on broccoli or carrots—there's just not enough profit in that," she says. "And they don't work on rice. It feeds half the world, but it doesn't feed the wealthy half."

Sitting in her eclectic, pesticide-free garden, she says rice could be the ideal proving ground for genetic engineering to improve the environment while preparing for a warmer world.

The Creation of Flood-Proof Rice

Take flooding, for instance. No one knows for certain how much flooding will increase as the planet warms, but scientists believe it will become more frequent and last longer in places such as Southeast Asia, where it already causes around $1 billion in annual damage to rice crops.

That's why Ronald's lab teamed up with colleague Dave Mackill in the late 1990s to create a species of rice that could be submerged for weeks during a flood and still survive. Unlike many crops, rice has a dizzying number of varieties (as many as 140,000), all with distinct genetic codes. Mackill had found one from eastern India with an unusual ability to live underwater for long spans. So Ronald's team undertook the painstaking task of sorting through the genome until they found a single gene that seemed to act as a "master switch" for flood tolerance.

It was a neat trick, but the researchers wanted something that could be used easily by poor rice farmers. One method would have been to slice the gene out and simply slide it into a commercial crop, making it "genetically modified." However, they finally decided to simply breed the old with the new while targeting that specific place in the gene that held the precious submergence trait. This so-called "marker-assisted" breeding blends genetic work with old-school, dirty-fingernails farming. Because the actual genetic transfer was done in rice fields rather than labs, the new strain is not considered modified and is thus under less scrutiny from government agencies.

In a 2006 paper in *Nature*, the team announced a new strain of rice that could survive two weeks totally underwater. What's more, it was easy to grow. By the end of this year [2010], the new, flood-proof rice will cover 125,000 acres in four countries. Next year that's projected to jump tenfold.

And Ronald says this is just the beginning. Flooding is one of climate change's three key threats to agriculture—drought and pest outbreaks are the other two—and Ronald believes lab-aided rice can be designed to resist them all. She is just beginning to work on drought-tolerant rice, and she believes a bug- and weed-resistant rice could slash the amount of pesticides rice farmers spew into the environment.

Genetic Engineering vs. Pesticides

For Ronald, it's an example of how genetic engineering has accomplished exactly what many environmentalists and organic farmers want. Genetically modified cotton is a prime example. Little more than a decade ago, farmers in China started using "Bt cotton," a genetically engineered variety containing a protein that kills pests but is nontoxic to mammals. (The Bt protein is a favorite insecticide among organic farmers.) Within four years, the Chinese cotton farmers reduced their annual use of poisonous insecticides by 70,000 metric tons—almost as much as is used in all of California each year.

Of course, not everyone agrees. Opponents of genetic engineering worry that GM food carries some still-undiscovered health risks or that it's just a tool for big corporations to sell more pesticides. And Doug Gurian-Sherman, with the Union of Concerned Scientists, worries that expensive GM research siphons money from less sexy techniques. He says he likes marker-led breeding but wants to see more money spent on organic techniques that reduce sprawling monocultures and mix together crops, more like a natural ecosystem.

For Ronald, the danger of pesticides far outweighs that of switching a few base pairs in the DNA. She frequently notes that there's no record of anyone ever becoming sick from a GM crop. On the other hand, pesticides kill 200 to 1,000 Americans a year, according to the World Health Organization.

A Debate of False Dichotomies

Ronald also points out that the debate over GM revolves around several false dichotomies. While naysayers declare genetic modification to be a new and evil practice, for example, Ronald says the line between "genetically engineered" and "traditional" crops really exists only in the media and politics. For scientists, she says, it's more of a continuum—with traditional breeding on one end and crops with genes borrowed from vastly different creatures on the other. "It's not the process that is good or bad, it's the product," she says.

Another false trade-off is the idea that embracing GM means doing away with other environmentally friendly agriculture practices. If we are to feed the world without destroying the planet, Ronald believes, we must incorporate not just GM but also many ideas promoted by organic farmers, such as crop rotations and crop diversity.

To explain what might finally tip the scales in GM's favor, Ronald points to the situation in the developing world. As global warming grinds forward, poor subsistence farmers will be devastated by food insecurity far more than the wealthy West. "If farmers don't change the seed they're planting now, in 25 years they're going to be getting half the yield," Ronald says. She believes altering rice and other crops—such as strains of bananas crucial to small African economies—could help prevent future famine, much in the way that Borlaug's wheat spared millions of people from starvation. If we're going to accomplish that, environmentalists need to think more broadly. "You don't have to choose between productivity and sustainability," she says, leaning back and looking around her eclectic garden. "You can have both."

VIEWPOINT 4

> *"The intrinsic yields of corn and soybeans did rise during the twentieth century, but not as a result of genetically engineered traits."*

Genetically Modified Crops Will Not Increase Productivity to End World Hunger

Union of Concerned Scientists

In the following viewpoint, the Union of Concerned Scientists argues that despite claims by the biotechnology industry that genetically engineered (GE) crops can increase yields, the data from the last several years does not support this claim. The Union of Concerned Scientists claims that the majority of increases in yields are not from genetic engineering and that it is nongenetic methods that ought to be pursued to increase future food production. The Union of Concerned Scientists is a science-based nonprofit group working for a healthy environment and a safer world.

As you read, consider the following questions:

1. According to the author, what are the two kinds of crop output measures?

"Failure to Yield: Biotechnology's Broken Promises," Union of Concerned Scientists Issue Briefing, July 2009, pp. 1–7.

2. According to the Union of Concerned Scientists, how much have wheat yields risen since the mid-1990s in absence of commercial genetic engineering?
3. According to the viewpoint, several international agencies have recommended that genetic engineering in developing countries play a secondary role to what?

There is a new urgency, prompted by recent spikes in food prices around the world, to boost global food production in order to feed a rapidly growing population. In response, the biotechnology industry has made optimistic claims about the ability of genetically engineered (GE) crops—in which the plant DNA is changed using spliced genes that are often from unrelated organisms—to substantially increase farmers' yields.

A Review of the Data

But are those claims valid? For the answer, the Union of Concerned Scientists carefully examined the industry's record in the United States, where GE crops have been commercially grown since the mid-1990s and where the best and most extensive data are available.

Because our focus was food production, we reviewed the data on soybeans and corn, the main GE food/feed crops. Soybeans engineered for herbicide tolerance currently account for more than 90 percent of all U.S. soybean acres planted, and GE corn makes up about 63 percent of the national corn crop. Within the GE corn varieties, some are engineered for herbicide tolerance; others contain genes from the *Bacillus thuringiensis* (Bt) bacterium, which render the plants resistant to several kinds of insect pests; and some have both types of genes. Now that these crops have been grown commercially for 13 years, there is a wealth of data on yield under well-controlled conditions. But our investigation of yield data for these GE crops shows that genetic engineering is not living up to its promise.

As described in our report, "Failure to Yield: Evaluating the Performance of Genetically Engineered Crops," we found that since the commercial introduction of GE food crops in the United States:

- Herbicide-tolerant (HT) GE soybeans and corn have not increased yields any more than conventional methods that rely on commonly available herbicides.
- Insect-resistant Bt corn varieties have provided an average yield advantage of just 3–4 percent compared to typical conventional practices, including synthetic insecticide use.
- Meanwhile, non-GE plant breeding and farming methods have increased yields of major grain crops by values ranging from 13–25 percent.

Two Kinds of Output Measures

There are two kinds of crop output measures: intrinsic yield and operational yield. Intrinsic yield reflects what could be achieved if crops were grown under ideal conditions; it also may be thought of as potential yield. By contrast, operational yield is what is obtained under actual conditions, where plants are subject to pests, drought stress, and other environmental factors. Genes that improve operational yield do so by reducing losses from such factors, but because they do not also increase potential yield they will probably not be sufficient to meet future food demand.

In examining the record of GE crops in raising both types of yield, we found:

1. Genetic engineering has not increased intrinsic yield.

No currently available GE varieties enhance the intrinsic yield of any crops. The intrinsic yields of corn and soybeans did rise during the twentieth century, but not as a result of GE traits. Rather, they were due to successes in traditional breeding.

2. Genetic engineering has delivered only minimal gains in operational yield.

The best available data suggest that HT soybeans and corn have not increased operational yields in the United States, whether on a per-acre or national basis, compared to conventional methods that rely on available herbicides.

Bt corn varieties, engineered to protect plants from either the European corn borer or corn rootworm, have fared better, but only slightly so. They provide an operational yield advantage of about 7–12 percent compared to typical conventional practices, including insecticide use—*but only when insect infestations are high*. Otherwise, Bt corn offers little or no advantage, even when compared to non-GE corn not treated with insecticides. Both varieties of Bt corn together provide an estimated operational yield increase of about 3–4 percent averaged across all corn acres, given that most corn acreage does not have high infestations of target insects. Averaged over the 13 years since 1996 (when Bt corn was first commercialized), this result amounts to about a 0.2–0.3 percent operational yield increase per year.

The Cause of Yield Gains

3. Most yield gains are attributable to nongenetic engineering approaches.

The biotechnology industry promotes the idea that GE technology has steadily increased U.S. farm productivity over the past 13 years. But while U.S. Department of Agriculture (USDA) data do show rising crop yields nationwide over that period, most of those gains cannot be attributed to the adoption of GE crops.

Take the case of corn, the most widely grown crop in the United States. Corn yields increased an average of about 1 percent per year over the last several decades of the twentieth century—considerably more in total than the yield increase

Rise in US Corn Yield Due to Genetic Engineering, Early 1990s to Present

Per-acre corn production in the United States has increased 28 percent since the early 1990s. Genetic engineering is responsible for only 14 percent of that increase (or 4 percent of total US yield increase); the majority of the increase is attributable to traditional breeding and other agricultural methods.

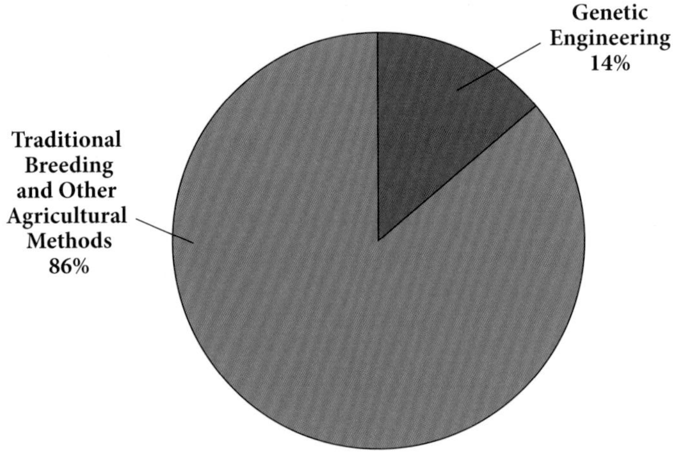

TAKEN FROM: Union of Concerned Scientists, "Failure to Yield: Biotechnology's Broken Promises," Issue Briefing, July 2009. www.ucsusa.org.

provided by Bt corn varieties. More recently, USDA data have indicated that the average corn production per acre nationwide over the past five years (2004–2008) was about 28 percent higher than for the five-year period 1991–1995, an interval that preceded the introduction of Bt varieties. But on the basis of our analysis of specific yield studies, we concluded that only 3–4 percent of that increase was attributable to Bt, meaning an increase of about 24–25 percent must have resulted from other factors, such as traditional breeding. No increase at all was attributable to GE HT corn.

Yields have also risen in other grain crops, but not because of GE. For example, total U.S. soybean yield has increased about 16 percent since the early to mid-1990s, yet our analysis of the data suggests that GE technology has produced neither intrinsic nor operational yield gains in commercialized varieties. Perhaps most striking is the case of wheat, where yields have risen 13 percent during this period of time, *in the absence of any commercially grown GE varieties.*

4. Experimental high-yield genetically engineered crops have not succeeded, despite considerable effort by the industry.

USDA records show that GE crop developers have applied to conduct thousands of experimental field trials since 1987. More than 650 of the applications specifically named yield as the target trait, while some 2,400 others listed target traits—including disease resistance and tolerance to environmental stresses such as drought, frost, flood, or saline soil—often associated with yield. But only the Bt and HT varieties discussed above, along with five disease-resistant varieties (grown on limited acreage), advanced from the experimental stage and are now being grown commercially. If the numerous other yield-enhancing test varieties were going to achieve results worthy of commercialization, at least some of them would have done so by now.

The Side Effects of Genetic Engineering

Engineering crops for increased yield is a difficult proposition. Unlike Bt and HT genes, most genes that control yield also influence many other genes. These complex genetic interactions typically have multiple effects on the plant, and early research is confirming that such effects can be detrimental. Even when the added yield-enhancing genes work as expected, they may diminish the crop's agricultural value in other ways.

In some cases, these genes may also have a variety of indirect but no less important impacts. Since their beginning, GE crops have sparked considerable public controversy, with critics warning of possible adverse health effects (including new allergies or toxicity when these foods are eaten), environmental impacts (such as the creation of new or more aggressive weeds), and economic outcomes (as in the contamination of other food crops with new genes). With their greater genetic complexity, crops specifically engineered for increased yield will likely present even more side effects, which will not always be identified under existing regulatory requirements. Thus, improved regulations will be needed to ensure that harmful side effects are discovered and prevented.

Alternatives Provide Greater Promise

GE crops have received huge investments of public and private research dollars since their introduction. Yet their minimal gains in yield stand in sharp contrast with the past gains and future potential of a suite of alternatives that require more modest initial investment and risk fewer potentially adverse impacts.

Traditional breeding has already proven itself capable of steadily increasing crop yields, and newer and more modern breeding methods are emerging. For example, high-tech genomic approaches (often called marker-assisted selection) use biotechnology—but not GE—to speed up the selection process for desired traits without actually inserting new genes from other species that could not mate with the crop. These approaches also have the potential to increase both intrinsic and operational yield.

Studies increasingly show the promise of agroecological farming methods. For example, farmers have long known that more extensive crop rotations, using a larger number of crops and longer rotations, can cut losses from insect pests and disease; such approaches also entail less reliance on pesticides than the corn/soybean rotations that currently dominate U.S. crop production. And research on low-external-input methods (which limit the use of synthetic fertilizers and pesticides) show that they can produce yields comparable to those of industrial-style conventional production methods. For example, non-GE soybeans in recent low-external-input U.S. experiments produced yields 13 percent higher than those of GE soybeans, although other low-external-input research and methods have shown lower yield.

The Need for a Sustainable Future

It is important to keep in mind where increased food production is most needed: in developing countries (especially in Africa) rather than in the developed world. Recent studies in these countries have shown that low-external-input methods can improve yield by more than 100 percent. And there are other benefits. Such methods are based largely on farmer knowledge rather than on costly inputs such as synthetic pesticides and GE seeds, and as a result they are often more accessible to poor farmers. Considering these advantages, a recent international assessment—supported by the World Bank, several United Nations agencies, numerous governments, several hundred scientists, and other experts—recommended that GE play a secondary role to organic and other low-external-input farming methods. The assessment also recommended improvements in infrastructure such as better water harvesting and grain storage and the building of new roads for market access.

While the need to increase food production is expected to become more urgent, awareness of the complex interactions between agriculture and the environment is also on the rise. Many of the predicted negative effects of global warming—including greater incidence and severity of extreme heat, drought, flooding, and sea-level rise (which may swamp coastal farmland)—are likely to make food production more challenging. At the same time, it is becoming clear that the past century's industrial methods of agriculture have imposed tremendous costs on our environment. For example, conventional agriculture contributes more heat-trapping emissions to the atmosphere than transportation, and it is a major source of water pollution that has led to large and spreading "dead zones" devoid of fish and shellfish (themselves important food sources) in the Gulf of Mexico and other bodies of water.

As the world strives to produce more food, it need not be at the expense of clean air, water, and soil and a stable climate. Instead, we must seek to achieve this goal efficiently and in ways that do not undermine the foundation of natural resources on which future generations will depend.

VIEWPOINT 5

"Responsible federal oversight of the fertility industry, in ways that protect reproductive rights and actually improve appropriate access to fertility treatment, is not only possible but long overdue."

Preventing the Next Fertility Clinic Scandal

Jesse Reynolds

In the following viewpoint, Jesse Reynolds argues that two recent scandals in the fertility industry illustrate the need for greater federal oversight of reproductive technologies. Reynolds claims that the existing self-regulation is currently not preventing doctors from implanting large numbers of embryos. Reynolds worries that the lack of oversight for the broadening use of genetic selection could result in a dangerous deepening of social prejudices against certain traits. Reynolds is a blogger who has written extensively on the social implications of biotechnology and is a former researcher at the Center for Genetics and Society.

As you read, consider the following questions:

1. According to the author, the Centers for Disease Control and Prevention (CDC) reports that what percentage of fertility clinics do not follow the implantation guidelines set by the industry itself?

Jesse Reynolds, "Preventing the Next Fertility Clinic Scandal," *Bioethics Forum*, March 13, 2009. Reproduced by permission.

2. Reynolds claims that a controversy recently erupted over a claim by a fertility doctor that there was pending availability of genetic selection for what three traits?
3. For what reason does Reynolds claim that achieving good legislation governing the fertility industry is a hazardous process?

Given the U.S. fertility industry's long-standing resistance to effective oversight, the field's two recent controversies—first octuplets, then an offer of embryo screening for cosmetic traits—shouldn't really come as a surprise. What was remarkable about the reaction they evoked from knowledgeable observers, in fact, was the chorus of agreement that it's time to leave the "Wild West" days of assisted reproduction behind.

The octuplets story turned many of us into reluctant voyeurs, fascinated by the daily dribble of details. Fortunately, at least some of the media attention soon turned away from the unsettling details about the babies' mother and focused instead on the fertility doctor involved. We soon learned that Michael Kamrava had not only transferred six embryos—two of which divided into twins—into the octuplets' mother, but had also recently put seven embryos into another woman who wanted only one child, leaving her pregnant with quadruplets.

The industry that had tolerated such irresponsible medical conduct also came under much-needed scrutiny. Many people were surprised to learn that the multibillion-dollar American fertility industry operates largely without oversight. It is subject only to the typical standards of general medical practice and the voluntary guidelines of the American Society for Reproductive Medicine (ASRM), the dominant industry group. The only federal requirement is for clinics to report their success rates to the Centers for Disease Control and Prevention (CDC).

How well does self-regulation work? Take the one guideline that has come under the most scrutiny: the number of embryos a fertility doctor should implant. The ASRM asks its members to transfer only one into women with a favorable prognosis who are under age 35 (as was the mother of octuplets). Yet CDC data reveal that the average number of embryos transferred is higher than the guideline. Media analysis of the CDC data shows that 80 percent of clinics do not follow the guidelines.

Although these guidelines are nonbinding, the ASRM and its sister organization, the Society for Assisted Reproductive Technology, could sanction members by expelling them. But that doesn't appear to be occurring. Our brief analysis found no correlation between whether a clinic meets the guideline and whether it is a member.

Condemnation of Kamrava came from all quarters: bioethicists, fertility doctors, users of assisted reproductive technologies, newspaper editorial boards, and "person on the street" interviews. And calls for regulation were unequivocal and frequent. An editorial in the *Los Angeles Times* said, "Clearly, the field of fertility treatment needs more than guidelines."

Bioethicist Art Caplan wrote in the *Philadelphia Inquirer*: "If the medical profession is unwilling or unable to police its own, then government needs to get involved. We already have rules governing who can get involved with adoption and foster care. Shouldn't these minimal requirements be extended to fertility treatment? And shouldn't some limit be set on how many embryos can be implanted at one time, along with some rules about what to do with embryos that no one wants to use?"

Other nations, such as Britain, keep a regulatory eye on reproductive technologies and those who wish to use them, knowing their use can put kids at risk in ways that nature never envisioned. We owe the same to children born here.

"There once was a lady who lived in a shoe . . . ," cartoon by Ann Telnaes. © 2009 Ann Telnaes. Used with the permission of Ann Telnaes and the Cartoonist Group.

A rare public defender of Kamrava was Dr. Jeffrey Steinberg, who said, "Who am I to say that six is the limit? There are people who like to have big families." In fact, he is at the center of the second recent controversy in the fertility industry.

For years, Steinberg has vocally supported broadening the use of genetic selection during IVF, or preimplantation genetic diagnosis (PGD), to any potential trait. He believes that "the ability of PGD should go as far as the science allows us to take it." Last December, his clinic's website began to advertise the "pending availability" of PGD for selection of the hair color, eye color, and skin color of future children. He dismissed criticism, noting that what he's offering is little different from existing procedures for adults: "I live in L.A. and everyone here wants to have a straight nose and high cheekbones and are perfectly happy to pay for cosmetic surgery."

Steinberg's offer was a realization of previous concerns about PGD. Predictions previously considered alarmist—"What's next . . . hair and eye color?"—were suddenly coming true. And the inclusion of skin complexion among the selectable traits holds the risk of reinvigorating our worst prejudices. As my colleague Osagie Obasogie wrote on the potential to scientifically influence skin color in *New Scientist* in 2007:

> As the science advances, however, policy makers must develop a regulatory framework that does not allow innovations to exploit the deep-rooted bias that society has towards certain groups. It would surely be a pity for any aspect of biotechnology research to develop in ways that help people to profit from racial prejudice.

After Steinberg's offer was reported in the *Wall Street Journal*, media coverage gradually grew. Three weeks after the *Journal* article, the story made it to the major television broadcast networks and cable news programs. Steinberg remained dismissive of concerns, and was the beneficiary of publicity via the controversy.

As with Kamrava's octuplets, criticism was widespread. Mark Hughes, a pioneer of PGD, said, "It's ridiculous and irresponsible . . . no legitimate lab would get into it and, if they did, they'd be ostracized." William Kearns, the medical geneticist on whose work Steinberg's procedure is based, was clear where he stood: "I won't sell my soul for any amount. Steinberg has jumped on my research but I'm totally against this." A father of one of the first children born via PGD, for a medical reason, wrote in a *Los Angeles Times* op-ed that, "Abusing that hard-won knowledge to capriciously choose hair color, eye color and other cosmetic traits in a baby is wrong and repugnant."

Art Caplan captured the concerns of many when he said, "Designing your descendents and seeking out perfection is the biggest slippery slope we could go on. Are the rich going to be able to do it and the poor not? Are we going to create a sort of subpopulation of the genetically perfect as against everybody else?" And Pamela Madsen, founder of the American Fertility Association, admitted:

> As a leading fertility advocate for close to 20 years, I have actively fought against federal legislation of reproductive technologies. But if the doctors in our field cannot employ common sense—and harness in their own—the time has never been riper for the federal government to step in.

Last week, Steinberg announced that he was suspending his program of trait selection, citing "apparent negative societal impacts." However, his statement was worded in a way that leaves the door open for later resumption.

If Steinberg does not resume offering so-called "designer babies," in the absence of clear lines, someone else will. As long as the baby business remains free of oversight, competitive pressures will push clinics into a race to the bottom, and social pressures will push parents to demand "only the best children."

However, achieving good legislation governing the fertility industry is a hazardous process. Some will try slipping Trojan horses that infringe on reproductive rights into proposals to regulate assisted reproduction. This is already occurring in Georgia, where legislators opposed to abortion rights introduced a bill that establishes the embryo as a person and likely prohibits the derivation of embryonic stem cell lines.

In contrast, in Missouri, a very brief bill simply limits the number of transferred embryos to what's specified in the ASRM guidelines. In fact, the industry group is supporting the measure. While it is a limited start, it demonstrates the principle that such proposals need not get entangled in abortion politics.

Yet state-level action can only go so far, and can actually be counterproductive. At their best, state laws will produce a cumbersome patchwork while encouraging fertility practitioners and patients to travel to the most favorable jurisdiction.

Responsible federal oversight of the fertility industry, in ways that protect reproductive rights and actually improve appropriate access to fertility treatment, is not only possible but long overdue. Most of the industrialized world has put such regulation and oversight in place. Comprehensive policies have been adopted in Canada, the United Kingdom, and elsewhere. It's time for the United States to catch up and move beyond its reputation as the "Wild West" of assisted reproduction.

Viewpoint 6

"Freedom from government interference has allowed geneticists to develop procedures that have resulted in thousands of healthy pregnancies since the early 1990s."

Society Could Benefit from Allowing Unregulated Embryo Trait Selection

Greg Beato

In the following viewpoint, Greg Beato argues that recent public outcry over genetic selection in embryos for nonmedical purposes is misguided. Beato denies that choosing traits is a shallow parental decision or that the practice would necessarily cause a genetic divide between rich and poor. He claims that allowing genetic reproductive technology to develop without government interference has resulted in many benefits for society, and there is no reason to think regulation is needed now. Beato is a writer based in San Francisco.

As you read, consider the following questions:

1. The author claims that for two decades fertility specialists have used genetic diagnosis to screen for what kinds of traits?

Greg Beato, "Billion Dollar Babies: The Brave New World of Designer Children," Reason.com, March 24, 2009. Reproduced by permission.

2. Why does Beato think that the analogy comparing trait selection to ordering take-out food speaks in favor of the practice rather than against it?

3. Why does the author think that even if genetic selection is used more often by the rich, this would still have positive effects on society?

Remember when the desktop publishing revolution gave anyone armed with a LaserWriter the power to design posters, brochures, and various other printed matter that had once been left to trained professionals? A tsunami of mismatched typefaces and ugly clip art was unleashed upon an unsuspecting world, and for many years, it was unsafe to look at the company newsletter without risking permanent retinal damage. So imagine what will happen when we all have the power to create our own highly customized designer babies.

A Customer-Oriented Approach

In February [2009], we took one short-lived baby step closer to that scenario. That's when Dr. Jeff Steinberg, director of the Fertility Institutes, a private medical practice with offices in Los Angeles, New York, and Mexico, told the *Wall Street Journal* about his plans to offer parents more aesthetic control over the manufacture of their offspring. A couple would specify their choices of hair color, eye color, and skin tone, and then, using an established procedure known as preimplantation genetic diagnosis (PGD), the Fertility Institutes would identify which of the parents' in vitro embryos were most likely to produce a child with those traits. The process wouldn't be foolproof, Dr. Steinberg qualified, but parents who employed it would substantially increase their chances of getting the baby of their dreams. The Fertility Institutes began promoting this pending service on its website in December; Dr. Steinberg told the *Journal* that about "half a dozen" clients had inquired about the service since then.

For nearly two decades, fertility specialists have used PGD to screen embryos for cystic fibrosis, hemophilia, and other genetic diseases. It can also be used simply for sex selection, and many clinics now offer this service. Dr. Steinberg's Fertility Institutes is one of them. On its website, it bills itself as "the world's leading center for 100% gender selection." Employing tactics more commonly associated with car dealerships and Vegas casinos, it also offers "low-interest 100% financing" and discounted travel packages that include airline tickets, hotel reservations, transportation, entertainment, dining, and child care services.

That's a refreshingly customer-oriented approach, but in the world of cutting-edge medicine, giving customers what they ask for is not always considered a virtue. While PGD in the service of avoiding disease has achieved widespread acceptance, PGD in the service of aesthetics and nonmedical screening is a lot more controversial. "This is cosmetic medicine," Dr. Steinberg told the *Journal*. "Others are frightened by the criticism but we have no problems with it." In a subsequent interview on CBS, he echoed these sentiments: "I think it's very important that we not bury our head in the sand and pretend these advances are not happening."

The Outcry over Genetic Selection

As Dr. Steinberg's plans to offer trait selection to prospective parents attracted more and more media coverage, however, he was subjected to more and more criticism. Some genetic experts said he couldn't deliver what he was promising. Others said he shouldn't. On March 2, just two weeks after the *Wall Street Journal* article ran, Dr. Steinberg aborted his plan to offer this new service: "In response to feedback received related to our plans to introduce preimplantation genetic prediction of eye pigmentation, an internal, self-regulatory decision has been made to proceed no further with this project," a statement on his website read. "Though well intended, we remain sensitive to public perception and feel that any benefit the diagnostic studies may offer are far outweighed by the apparent negative societal impacts involved." According to his publicist, Dr. Steinberg has no interest in commenting any further on the subject.

But even if Dr. Steinberg's head is now firmly buried in the sand, his words continue to resonate: These advances are happening. There are parents who'd like to utilize such services. If we are generally in favor of using PGD for medical reasons—of course, many people object to even this sort of usage—why are we so wary of extending the technology even further?

Media coverage of Dr. Steinberg's proposed trait selection service typically adopted a gently proscriptive tone. The *New York Daily News*, for example, likened it to building a customizable teddy bear. Todayshow.com compared it to ordering take-out food. The obvious question underlying these analogies: How can we treat creating a child as trivially and superficially as we treat buying fast-food via the drive-thru window? This question can easily be reversed, however: Why are so many of us content to exercise more control over our most quotidian consumer choices than we are over the most consequential decision we can make as humans? Could it be that parents determined to micromanaging their progeny's eye color are the ones who care the most?

The Worry of a Genetic Divide

Of course, it's not merely the prospect of green-eyed tots with complementary skin tones (and merely average brainpower) that keep transhumanists, bioethicists, and Hollywood screenwriters up at night. Eventually, genetic engineers will figure out ways to not only screen genes for mutations, but also to alter them in ways that increase intelligence or musical aptitude, augment height, amplify specific personality traits, et cetera. At that point, a new age of reproduction will be upon us, with parents eagerly designing a new generation of super babies with all the latest bells and whistles.

If they have the money to pay for such services, that is. Critics believe a "genetic divide" will eventually develop: While the rich fortify their heirs with the best genes money can buy, the poor will be stuck playing the genetic lottery. Eventually, life on earth will devolve into a massive reality series, with a ragtag tribe of Average Joes pitted against an invincible army of genius supermodel millionaires.

But are we really so sure that this is how it's going to play out? Think of the smartest people you know—are they also the richest people you know? Enhancing our wealthiest embryos with extra IQ points and superior athletic skills may simply lead to a lot of investment bankers bitterly disappointed in how their son the anthropology professor/yoga instructor turned out.

In addition, what's better for society in the long run—smart rich people or dumb rich people? Maybe Bill Gates's designer baby will grow up to discover a way to make gene enhancement more affordable. Maybe he'll also set up a foundation that offers gene enhancement "scholarships" to families who would otherwise not be able to obtain these services.

The Danger of Government Interference

One thing we know about humans: They behave in unpredictable ways. They use new technologies in ways the inventors of those technologies never imagined. At this point, when we haven't even discovered what kind of cultural impact giving parents the ability to choose their child's eye color might have, how can we know what it is about next-stage designer babies that we're trying to protect ourselves from?

As the *Wall Street Journal* reported, PGD is currently "unfettered by any state or federal regulations in the U.S." That freedom from government interference has allowed geneticists to develop procedures that have resulted in thousands of healthy pregnancies since the early 1990s. As the potential for aesthetic and nonmedical genetic screening grows more concrete, however, opposition to PGD and related technologies is manifesting itself at the legislative level. A few weeks ago in Georgia, for example, the state senate passed a bill that appears to make PGD illegal—its text reserves embryo "solely for the purposes of initiating a human pregnancy by means of transfer to the uterus of a human female for the treatment of human infertility." The Center for Genetics and Society is calling for congressional hearings regarding the fertility industry. According to *Slate*'s William Saletan, these efforts mark the beginning of "a nationwide project to regulate the emerging industry of embryo production." For anyone who believes not only in the possibilities of extending reproductive options, but merely protecting the ones we currently enjoy, it is no time to have one's head in the sand.

Periodical and Internet Sources Bibliography

The following articles have been selected to supplement the diverse views presented in this chapter.

Terra Brockman	"Fooling the World, Not Feeding It," Zester Daily, June 16, 2010. www.zesterdaily.com.
Gregory Conko and Henry I. Miller	"The Rush to Condemn Genetically Modified Crops," *Policy Review*, no. 165, February/March 2011.
Peter Dizikes	"Your DNA Is a Snitch," *Salon*, February 17, 2009.
Bill Freese	"Biotech Snake Oil: A Quack Cure for Hunger," *Multinational Monitor*, September/October 2008.
Hans Herren and Marcia Ishii-Eiteman	"Genetically Modified Crops Are Not the Answer," *Hill*, April 22, 2010.
Ari Levaux	"The Very Real Danger of Genetically Modified Foods," *Atlantic*, January 9, 2012.
Erin Nelson and Timothy Caulfield	"When It Comes to 'Saviour Siblings,' Let's Just Stick to the Facts," *Globe and Mail* (Canada), June 24, 2009.
Leslie A. Pray	"Embryo Screening and the Ethics of Human Genetic Engineering," *Nature Education*, 2008.
Julian Savulescu	"Breeding Perfect Babies," *The Drum Opinion*, November 12, 2008.
Wesley J. Smith	"'Savior Siblings' Start Us Down Harrowing Ethical Path," *National Review Online*, March 2, 2011.
Bonnie Steinbock	"Designer Babies: Choosing Our Children's Genes," *Lancet*, October 11, 2008.

OPPOSING VIEWPOINTS® SERIES

Chapter 3

What Is the Environmental Impact of Genetic Engineering?

Chapter Preface

The environmental impact of the use of genetic engineering technologies is open to debate. On the one hand, proponents claim as the justification for the use of many of the technologies that they can improve the condition of the environment. On the other hand, opponents argue that genetic technologies will harm the environment on balance. The use of genetic engineering in crops such as corn, soy, and cotton is one area of use that is fraught with conflicting points of view.

Common genetically modified crops include the *Bacillus thuringiensis* (Bt) crops that synthesize their own bacteria to kill pests and herbicide-resistant crops that allow farmers to use herbicides without harming the crops. The use of these genetically modified crops has been credited with reducing the release of greenhouse gas emissions in two ways. First, less fuel is used for herbicide and pesticide application. Second, more carbon remains stored in the soil, rather than released into the atmosphere, because better weed control means less tilling of the soil. According to one worldwide study, from 1996 to 2010 the cumulative permanent reduction of fuel use resulting from less frequent herbicide or insecticide applications with genetically modified crops was estimated at 12,232 million kilograms of carbon dioxide, equal to removing 760,000 cars from the road for one year.[1] According to the study, the use of genetically modified soybeans in the United States alone resulted in reduced fuel use equal to 246 million kilograms of carbon dioxide, or the removal of 109,000 cars from the road for one year. The study estimates that due to

1. Graham Brookes and Peter Barfoot, "GM Crops: Global Socio-Economic and Environmental Impacts 1996–2010," PG Economics Ltd, UK, May 2012.

reduced tillage of genetically modified crops, an additional carbon dioxide savings of 133,639 million kilograms has occurred since 1996.

Not everyone agrees that genetically modified crops have been good for the environment, however. Greenpeace warns that Bt crops that kill pests, resulting in the need to use fewer pesticides, have their own environmental dangers. The organization claims that the toxins secreted by Bt crops not only kill the target species but also induce adverse effects on nontarget species such as the monarch butterfly and beneficial insects such as the honeybee. Greenpeace also warns that the residues left in the soil from Bt crops pose unknown risks to the long-term health of the soil and to aquatic life. Furthermore, the organization expresses concern about genetically modifying crops for herbicide tolerance, claiming that the use of herbicides poses risks for several organisms in the environment. Research in 2012 found that herbicide-resistant weeds are driving up the volume of herbicide needed to grow genetically modified crops:

> Herbicide-resistant crop technology has led to a 239 million kilogram (527 million pound) increase in herbicide use in the United States between 1996 and 2011, while Bt crops have reduced insecticide applications by 56 million kilograms (123 million pounds). Overall, pesticide use increased by an estimated 183 million kilograms (404 million pounds), or about 7%.[2]

This research concludes that there are grave concerns about the continued increased need for herbicides with genetically modified crops.

Genetically modified crops have the potential to result in environmental benefits by reducing the need for pesticide use and reducing the amount of carbon dioxide emitted through farming practices. However, genetic engineering of crops also

2. Charles M. Benbrook, "Impacts of Genetically Engineered Crops on Pesticide Use in the U.S.—the First Sixteen Years," *Environmental Sciences Europe*, vol. 24, 2012.

runs the risk of creating new environmental problems, many of which may not emerge until the technology has been used for some time. Determining the overall impact of genetically engineered crops on the environment is one of the many considerations that will affect the future use of this technology for food production.

Viewpoint 1

"Because we believe that mitigating climate change can help a great many people, we see human engineering in this context as an ethical endeavor."

Human Genetic Engineering Is a Good Solution to Climate Change

S. Matthew Liao, interviewed by Ross Andersen

In the following viewpoint, S. Matthew Liao, interviewed by Ross Andersen, argues that engineering the human body could help combat climate change. In addition to voluntary pharmaceutical engineering, he contends that genetic engineering could be used to make humans smaller in order to have less environmental impact. Liao contends that as long as the engineering is voluntary, it could actually enhance an individual's liberty while also helping the environment. Liao is director of the bioethics program and associate professor in the Center for Bioethics at New York University. Andersen is a correspondent for the Atlantic.

S. Matthew Liao, interviewed by Ross Andersen, "How Engineering the Human Body Could Combat Climate Change," *The Atlantic*, March 12, 2012.

As you read, consider the following questions:

1. The author cites a UN Food and Agriculture Organization report that estimates what percentage of the world's greenhouse gas emissions and CO_2 equivalents come from livestock farming?

2. How could human engineering result in more choice for families regarding family size, according to Liao?

3. Liao hypothesizes that people might resist the idea of having shorter children for what reason?

The threat of global climate change has prompted us to redesign many of our technologies to be more energy efficient. From lightweight hybrid cars to long-lasting LEDs [light-emitting diodes], engineers have made well-known products smaller and less wasteful. But tinkering with our tools will only get us so far, because however smart our technologies become, the human body has its own ecological footprint, and there are more of them than ever before. So, some scholars are asking, what if we could engineer *human beings* to be more energy efficient? A new paper to be published in *Ethics, Policy & Environment* proposes a series of biomedical modifications that could help humans, themselves, consume less.

Some of the proposed modifications are simple and non-invasive. For instance, many people wish to give up meat for ecological reasons, but lack the willpower to do so on their own. The paper suggests that such individuals could take a pill that would trigger mild nausea upon the ingestion of meat, which would then lead to a lasting aversion to meat eating. Other techniques are bound to be more controversial. For instance, the paper suggests that parents could make use of genetic engineering or hormone therapy in order to birth smaller, less resource-intensive children.

The Problem of Climate Change

The lead author of the paper, S. Matthew Liao, is a professor of philosophy and bioethics at New York University. Liao is keen to point out that the paper is not meant to advocate for any particular human modifications, or even human engineering generally; rather, it is only meant to introduce human engineering as one possible, partial solution to climate change. He also emphasized the voluntary nature of the proposed modifications. Neither Liao nor his coauthors, Anders Sandberg and Rebecca Roache of Oxford, approve of any coercive human engineering; they favor modifications borne of individual choices, not technocratic mandates. What follows is my conversation with Liao about why he thinks human engineering could be the most ethical and effective solution to global climate change.

[Ross Andersen:] Judging from your paper, you seem skeptical about current efforts to mitigate climate change, including market-based solutions like carbon pricing or even more radical solutions like geoengineering. Why is that?

[S. Matthew Liao:] It's not that I don't think that some of those solutions could succeed under the right conditions; it's more that I think that they might turn out to be inadequate, or in some cases too risky. Take market solutions—so far it seems like it's pretty difficult to orchestrate workable international agreements to affect international emissions trading. The Kyoto Protocol [an international agreement on climate change], for instance, has not produced demonstrable reductions in global emissions, and in any event demand for petrol and for electricity seems to be pretty inelastic. And so it's questionable whether carbon taxation alone can deliver the kind of reduction that we need to really take on climate change.

With respect to geoengineering, the worry is that it's just too risky—many of the technologies involved have never been attempted on such a large scale, and so you have to worry that by implementing these techniques we could endanger ourselves or future generations. For example it's been suggested that we could alter the reflectivity of the atmosphere using sulfate aerosol so as to turn away a portion of the sun's heat, but it could be that doing so would destroy the ozone layer, which would obviously be problematic. Others have argued that we ought to fertilize the ocean with iron, because doing so might encourage a massive bloom of carbon-sucking plankton. But doing so could potentially render the ocean inhospitable to fish, which would obviously also be quite problematic.

A Plan to Reduce Meat Consumption

One human engineering strategy you mention is a kind of pharmacologically induced meat intolerance. You suggest that humans could be given meat alongside a medication that triggers extreme nausea, which would then cause a long-lasting aversion to meat eating. Why is it that you expect this could have such a dramatic impact on climate change?

There is a widely cited UN [United Nations] Food and Agriculture Organization report that estimates that 18% of the world's greenhouse gas emissions and CO_2 equivalents come from livestock farming, which is actually a much higher share than from transportation. More recently it's been suggested that livestock farming accounts for as much as 51% of the world's greenhouse gas emissions. And then there are estimates that as much as 9% of human emissions occur as a result of deforestation for the expansion of pastures for livestock. And that doesn't even take into account the emissions that arise from manure, or from the livestock directly. Since a large portion of these cows and other grazing animals are raised for consumption, it seems obvious that reducing the consumption of these meats could have considerable environmental benefits.

Even a minor 21% to 24% reduction in the consumption of these kinds of meats could result in the same reduction in emissions as the total localization of food production, which would mean reducing "food miles" to zero. And, I think it's important to note that it wouldn't necessarily need to be a pill. We have also toyed around with the idea of a patch that might stimulate the immune system to reject common bovine proteins, which could lead to a similar kind of lasting aversion to meat products.

The Size of Humans

Your paper also discusses the use of human engineering to make humans smaller. Why would this be a powerful technique in the fight against climate change?

Well one of the things that we noticed is that human ecological footprints are partly correlated with size. Each kilogram of body mass requires a certain amount of food and nutrients and so, other things being equal, [the] larger the person is the more food and energy they are going to soak up over the course of a lifetime. There are also other, less obvious ways in which larger people consume more energy than smaller people—for example a car uses more fuel per mile to carry a heavier person, more fabric is needed to clothe larger people, and heavier people wear out shoes, carpets and furniture at a quicker rate than lighter people, and so on.

And so size reduction could be one way to reduce a person's ecological footprint. For instance if you reduce the average U.S. height by just 15cm [centimeters], you could reduce body mass by 21% for men and 25% for women, with a corresponding reduction in metabolic rates by some 15% to 18%, because less tissue means lower energy and nutrient needs.

What are the various ways humans could be engineered to be smaller?

There are a couple of ways, actually. You might try to do it through a technique called preimplantation genetic diagnosis, which is already used in IVF [in vitro fertilization] settings in

The Malleability of People's Attitudes

What may be unappealing today may not be so tomorrow. This could be because people's attitudes about what is appealing can and do change, especially if there are ethical reasons for a particular type of intervention. For example, people's attitudes towards vegetarianism have changed as a result of vegetarianism's ethical status. People's attitudes toward currently unappealing human engineering solutions may undergo a similar change as awareness spreads about the effects that these solutions could have on the problem of climate change. Our attitudes about the extent to which certain qualities are appealing can also change with changes in the people around us. A recent study shows that those who care about their weight are more likely to allow themselves to grow fatter when surrounded by overweight people than they are when surrounded by slim people. This suggests that, even if a relatively small number of people made their children smaller, this might result in a reduction in the extent to which having a certain minimum height is valued by others. With the right incentives, such as tax breaks, those others might be willing to have smaller children of their own.

S. Matthew Liao, Anders Sandberg, and Rebecca Roache, "Human Engineering and Climate Change," Ethics, Policy & Environment, *vol. 15, no. 2, 2012.*

fertility clinics today. In this scenario you'd be looking to select which embryos to implant based on height.

Another way to affect height is to use a hormone treatment to trigger the closing of the epiphyseal plate earlier than normal—this sometimes happens by accident in vitamin overdose cases. In fact hormone treatments are already used for height reduction in overly tall children. A final way you could do this is by way of gene imprinting, by influencing the competition between maternal and paternal genes, where there is a height disparity between the mother and father. You could have drugs that reduce or increase the expression of paternal or maternal genes in order to affect birth height.

Human Engineering and Liberty

Isn't it ethically problematic to allow parents to make these kinds of irreversible choices for their children?

That's a really good question. First, I think it's useful to distinguish between selection and modification. With selection you don't really have the issue of irreversible choices because the embryo selected can't complain that she could have been otherwise—if the parents had selected a different embryo, she wouldn't have existed at all. In the case of modification, that issue could certainly arise, but even then I think it's important to step back and ask why we are looking at these solutions in the first place. The reason we are even considering these solutions is to prevent climate change, which is a really serious problem, and which might affect the well-being of millions of people including the child. And so in that context, if on balance human engineering is going to promote the well-being of that particular child, then you might be able to justify the solution to the child. . . .

In your paper you suggest that some human engineering solutions may actually be liberty enhancing. How so?

That's right. It's been suggested that, given the seriousness of climate change, we ought to adopt something like China's one-child policy. There was a group of doctors in Britain who recently advocated a two-child maximum. But at the end of the day those are crude prescriptions—what we really care about is some kind of fixed allocation of greenhouse gas emissions per family. If that's the case, given certain fixed allocations of greenhouse gas emissions, human engineering could give families the choice between two medium-sized children, or three small-sized children. From our perspective, that would be more liberty enhancing than a policy that says "you can only have one or two children." A family might want a really good basketball player, and so they could use human engineering to have one really large child.

I have to push back a little on that point. It seems like those human engineering techniques would be liberty enhancing only in a context in which there were some severe liberty constraint that doesn't exist now. Is there another way these techniques might be liberty enhancing?

Well, again, I would return to the weakness of will consideration. If you crave steak, and that craving prevents you from making a decision you otherwise want to make, in some sense your inability to control yourself is a limit on the will, or a limit on your liberty. A meat patch would allow you to truly decide whether you want to have that steak or not, and that could be quite liberty enhancing.

Opposition to Human Engineering

Your paper focuses on human engineering techniques that are relatively safe. Did your research lead you to any interesting techniques that were unsafe?

Actually, yes, although unfortunately the science is not there yet—we looked into cat eyes, the technique of giving humans cat eyes or of making their eyes more catlike. The reason is, cat eyes see nearly as well as human eyes during the day, but much better at night. We figured that if everyone had cat eyes, you wouldn't need so much lighting, and so you could reduce global energy usage considerably. Maybe even by a shocking percentage.

But, again, this isn't something we know how to do yet, although it's possible there might be some way to do it with genetics—there are some primates with eyes that are very similar to cat eyes, and so possibly we could study those primates and figure out which genes are responsible for that trait, and then hopefully activate those genes in humans. But that's very speculative and requires a lot of research.

Some critics are likely to see these techniques as inappropriately interfering with human nature. What do you say to them?

Well, first, I would say that the view that you shouldn't interfere with human nature at all is too strong. For instance, giving women epidurals when they're giving birth is in some sense interfering with human nature, but it's generally welcomed. Also, when people worry about interfering with human nature, they generally worry about interfering for the wrong reasons. But because we believe that mitigating climate change can help a great many people, we see human engineering in this context as an ethical endeavor, and so that objection may not apply.

In your paper you argue that some of the initial opposition to these solutions is rooted in a particular kind of status quo bias. Can you explain what you mean by that?

Sure. Take having smaller children for example. People might resist this idea because they might think that there is some sort of optimal—the average height in a given society, say. But, I think it's worth remembering how fluid human traits like height are. A hundred years ago people were much shorter on average, and there was nothing wrong with them medically. And so, if people are resistant to the idea of engineering humans to be smaller because of some notion of an optimal height, they might be operating from a status quo bias.

Taking a look at this from the perspective of deep ecology—is there something to be said for the idea that because climate change is human caused, that humans ought to be the ones that change to mitigate it—that somehow we ought to bear the cost to fix this?

That was actually one of the ideas that motivated us to write this paper, the idea that we caused anthropogenic climate change, and so perhaps we ought to bear some of the costs required to address it. But having said that, we also want to make this attractive to people—we don't want this to be a zero-sum game where it's just a cost that we have to bear. Many of the solutions we propose might actually be quite desirable to people, particularly the meat patch. I recently gave a talk about this paper at Yale and there was a man in the audience who worked for a pharmaceuticals company; he seemed to think there might be a huge market for modifications like this.

Viewpoint 2

> *"These bioethicists themselves may not be totalitarian, but there are plenty of radical environmentalists who are, and who take such ideas seriously."*

Human Genetic Engineering Is a Dangerous Proposal to Combat Climate Change

Mark Tapson

In the following viewpoint, Mark Tapson argues that the proposal to genetically engineer humans in order to address climate change is frightening. Tapson rejects the idea that submitting to genetic engineering would be liberty enhancing and suggests that the notion that such intervention would be voluntary is an illusion. In addition, Tapson questions the idea that climate change is man-made and that humans have a duty to address it. Tapson is a Hollywood-based writer and screenwriter, as well as a Shillman Journalism Fellow at the David Horowitz Freedom Center.

As you read, consider the following questions:

1. The author responds to a proposal to address global warming that he says involves more radical sacrifices than what current practices?

Mark Tapson, "Let's Get Small," *FrontPage Mag*, April 2, 2012.

2. Tapson implies that the option of what three choices under the human engineering proposal for climate change actually is not very liberty enhancing?
3. Tapson claims that typical liberal academics operate from a standpoint involving what three assumptions?

The man-made global warming alarmists now suspect that all our efforts to reverse imminent planetary disaster may be inadequate and ultimately futile. Always thinking outside the box, they're suggesting more radical sacrifices than simply upgrading lightbulbs and trading in gas-guzzlers for Priuses. Forget *badgering* people to be more energy efficient, some global warming strategists are asking why not *genetically alter* them to be so? "Let's get small" doesn't refer just to Steve Martin's old comedy routine anymore; now it's a call to bioengineer *smaller humans* for a reduced carbon footprint.

In an online interview for the *Atlantic*, S. Matthew Liao, professor of philosophy and bioethics at New York University, expresses skepticism about the efficacy of our current attempts to mitigate climate change, and theorizes that "voluntary" human engineering is one possible solution. He is the principal author of the new paper "Human Engineering and Climate Change," in the scholarly journal *Ethics, Policy & Environment*. In it, he and his coauthors propose possible biomedical modifications to ensure that humans tread less heavily on Mother Gaia.

The Human Engineering Proposals

For example, Liao says reducing our consumption of meat could have significant environmental benefits. One solution could be a pill that triggers mild nausea upon the ingestion of meat and ultimately creates in us an aversion to meat altogether. Other techniques are more complicated both medically and ethically; Liao and his cohorts even considered the possibility, for example, of giving humans "cat eyes":

> The reason is, cat eyes see nearly as well as human eyes during the day, but much better at night. We figured that if everyone had cat eyes, you wouldn't need so much lighting, and so you could reduce global energy usage considerably.

Then there is the issue of our inconvenient physical size:

> [The] larger a person is the more food and energy they are going to soak up over the course of a lifetime. There are also other, less obvious ways in which larger people consume more energy than smaller people—for example a car uses more fuel per mile to carry a heavier person, more fabric is needed to clothe larger people, and heavier people wear out shoes, carpets and furniture at a quicker rate than lighter people, and so on.

In order to reduce a person's environmental footprint substantially, then, Liao and his partners theorize that parents might submit to genetic engineering or hormone therapy in order to give birth to smaller, "less resource-intensive" children. The authors believe that such human engineering solutions may actually be "liberty enhancing," especially in contrast to "crude prescriptions" like China's "one-child" policy:

> What we really care about is some kind of fixed allocation of greenhouse gas emissions per family. If that's the case . . . human engineering could give families the choice between two medium-sized children, or three small-sized children. From our perspective that would be more liberty enhancing than a policy that says "you can only have one or two children." A family might want a really good basketball player, and so they could use human engineering to have one really large child.

The Issue of Liberty

That's the global warming community's concept of "liberty enhancing"—a population control policy that gives people the magnanimous option of three undersized children, two mediums, or one basketball player.

For those not enlightened enough to find this option appealing, these philosophers also discuss the "pharmacological enhancement" of qualities like empathy and altruism, traits that are more conducive to positive attitudes toward the environment. When the *Atlantic* interviewer questioned whether it isn't problematic to biologically produce a belief in a person, Liao corrects him; it's not about inserting a belief, it's about enabling people to overcome their "weakness of will" and make the right choice:

> We are interested only in voluntary modifications, and we certainly don't want to implant beliefs into anyone. But even then, those beliefs might still be considered yours if they arise from a kind of ramping up of your existing capacities, and so perhaps that could obviate that problem.

Neither he nor his colleagues approve of any coercive human engineering; they favor "individual choices, not technocratic mandates." Of course, it's not voluntary for the children whose parents have made such irreversible choices for them. But Liao points out that it's for their own good:

> The reason we are even considering these solutions is to prevent climate change, which is a really serious problem, and which might affect the well-being of millions of people including the child. And so in that context, if on balance human engineering is going to promote the well-being of that particular child, then you might be able to justify the solution to the child.

Regarding those who don't feel a thrill running up their leg at this idea, Liao dismisses such resistance as a natural sort of "status quo bias"; in other words, those people are simply clinging to old ways of thinking.

A Danger of Totalitarianism

The *Atlantic* interview sparked some online outrage from readers toward Liao and his coauthors, Oxford's Anders Sandberg and Rebecca Roache, for their eyebrow-raising proposals—the trio was compared to Nazi eugenicists, for example. In a separate interview about that reaction, the paper's authors hastened to reiterate, as Liao did in his interview, that they do not necessarily advocate such speculations. "Philosophers . . . spend a lot of time discussing views that they do not necessarily endorse," explained Roache. "It's part of the learning process."

Liao acknowledges that "our proposal to encourage having smaller, but environmentally friendlier human beings is *prima facie* outlandish," but points out that when we dismiss outlandish ideas too quickly, we may be leaving ourselves "vulnerable to dismissing useful and valuable" ones. Even the journal that published the paper described its ideas as "a series of Swiftian [referring to the satire of Jonathan Swift] philosophical thought experiments." "None of us are deep greens or totalitarian," added Sandberg. "We are fairly typical liberal academics thinking about the world."

When "typical liberal academics" start thinking about the world, beware. They operate from the assumption that man-made global warming is a fact, that humans are inherently detrimental to the planet, and that the right thing to do is to conform everything about our existence for the sake of Earth's ostensible well-being. That includes floating the idea of a "voluntary" reduction in the number and size of our children. These bioethicists themselves may not be totalitarian, but there are plenty of radical environmentalists who are, and who take such ideas seriously. You don't need cat's eyes to see the danger in that.

VIEWPOINT 3

"Sustainable aquaculture, based on responsible modern biology, including genetic engineering, will provide the world with the seafood that we need and help conserve our planet."

Genetically Engineered Fish Can Provide Food and Conserve the Planet

Yonathan Zohar

In the following viewpoint, Yonathan Zohar argues that the population of the world and an increased demand for fish make hunting for seafood in the wild unsustainable, necessitating the growth of aquaculture, or fish farming. Zohar claims that genetically engineered fish offer benefits to the aquaculture industry and are safe for consumers. Zohar concludes that as long as genetically engineered fish do not escape into the wild, they are a good solution to an environmental problem. Zohar is chair and professor of the Department of Marine Biotechnology at the University of Maryland.

Yonathan Zohar, "Genetically Modified Salmon Is Fit for the Table," CNN, September 22, 2010.

As you read, consider the following questions:

1. The author cites a study by the United Nations (UN) Food and Agriculture Organization showing that what percentage of stocks of the world's main fisheries are fully exploited?
2. Zohar claims that AquAdvantage salmon is genetically engineered in what way?
3. Zohar cautions that failing to label genetically engineered salmon as such would result in what harm?

The debate over genetically engineered salmon should be put in the proper context: As the world's population grows at an accelerating pace, so does the consumption of seafood.

This is true not only because there are more mouths to feed, but also because as people become more aware of the health benefits associated with eating seafood, more are switching from meat to fish. To satisfy this demand, we have become very sophisticated fishers, with ever-growing fleets, factory fishing ships and very effective gear.

The Need for Aquaculture

We efficiently hunt our own seafood in the wild; it seems natural to all of us, while we do not hunt for wild chicken, beef or pork. But fish is harvested at a rate that exceeds the fisheries' ability to replenish themselves.

According to the UN [United Nations] Food and Agriculture Organization, more than 50 percent of the world's main fisheries stocks are fully exploited, while another 28 percent are overexploited or depleted.

Fish species that used to be plentiful, such as cod, plaice, haddock and others, are now rare in the wild. The king of the oceans, the giant bluefin tuna, is now near the point of no return; its stocks dropping precipitously in the past decade alone.

Reflecting upon these declines, the U.S. has become the world's second-largest importer of seafood (after Japan) with more than 80 percent of the seafood consumed in this country coming from overseas. And seafood imports contribute $9 billion annually to the U.S. trade deficit, largest among all agricultural products.

Fisheries scientists have repeatedly warned us that if we do not change our commercial fisheries practices, we will run out of the vast majority of the commercial species by the middle of this century.

This must stop. Like any other animal or plant crop, fish and seafood must be produced through farming—or aquaculture—and the wild stocks should be protected so they can recover. As a society, we must accept that while it is nice to eat wild salmon, there is no wild Atlantic salmon out there; we must get used to eating farmed fish.

The Promise of Genetically Engineered Fish

The aquaculture industry faces a huge challenge. It must grow fish in a way that is economically viable and environmentally responsible. And this is where genetic engineering enters the picture. Genetically engineered fish, like the AquAdvantage salmon, offer great benefits to fish farmers and should be available to the industry.

If used carefully, genetic engineering can produce fish that reach the market much faster, as in the AquAdvantage salmon, and use less feed (and thus less fish meal).

As the science develops, it could generate fish that are resistant to disease (currently the aquaculture industry loses billions of dollars annually to disease in its fish population) and healthier for the consumer—making beneficial omega-3 oils available in fish that do not normally contain them, for example.

The public should not be scared by the term "genetic engineering." This powerful platform requires making only rela-

Top Importers of Fishery Commodities

Country or Area	Imports in US Dollars 2010
Korea Rep	3,191,371
Sweden	3,317,275
UK	3,714,443
Germany	5,026,193
Italy	5,419,750
France	5,975,261
China	6,157,028
Spain	6,512,081
Japan	14,891,698
USA	15,496,409

TAKEN FROM: Food and Agriculture Organization of the United Nations, "Fishery and Aquaculture Statistics," *FAO Yearbook 2010*. Rome: Food and Agriculture Organization of the United Nations, 2012.

tively minor and very targeted modifications to the animal genome, compared, for example, with selective breeding and domestication, where we manipulate many genes over generations without knowing exactly what is altered.

We have all been eating selectively bred fish, chicken, beef and other animals for many years without thinking twice about it. The AquAdvantage Atlantic salmon has only one extra copy of a fish gene inserted into its genome. This one addition, while enhancing the hormones of the growth axis in fish, operates within the fish's physiological range. And these are fish hormones that have no effect on the human consumer.

The AquAdvantage salmon is no different from conventional farmed salmon in its composition and health benefits, and the Food and Drug Administration [FDA] has concluded that it is safe for people to eat.

The Need to Contain Farmed Fish

The single most important caution I would offer is that we must ensure that these fish, as well as any other farmed but domesticated fish (non–genetically engineered), cannot escape from the farming systems to our seas or rivers.

The AquAdvantage salmon must be fully contained, both biologically and physically. Indeed, AquAdvantage salmon are sterile fish, and therefore unable to reproduce even if they escape. These fish are intended to be farmed only in fully contained, land-based farming systems. Every new operation that would grow these fish for sale in the United States would be subject to FDA approval, according to the FDA.

By using multiple and redundant mechanical means to prevent escape (such as screens and filters), as well as reusing the culture water, the systems should be close to full containment, having minimal interactions with the environment. And the implementation of these new, land-based and fully contained marine aquaculture systems offers an opportunity for aquaculture to become more efficient and environmentally sustainable.

However, before approving the genetically engineered fish for use in aquaculture, as a scientist, I would like to see the FDA and AquaBounty [Technologies] be less presumptive and more experimental about the potential environmental risk of AquAdvantage salmon.

I want to see scientific data, proof beyond a shadow of a doubt, that if fish do escape from containment, they will not survive, will not breed and will be purged from the environment. Experiments to demonstrate this are all feasible, but will take a few more years to complete.

The Need to Label Genetically Engineered Salmon

And finally, consumers should absolutely be informed whether the salmon they are buying is genetically engineered or not. It is our responsibility to make sure the public is educated so the fear factor dissipates and the consumer can make rational decisions regarding genetically engineered salmon. Not labeling the fish will harm the industry altogether as people who do not want genetically engineered fish will avoid farmed salmon altogether.

As a society that is in dire need of more plentiful and healthier food, we must accept the practices of modern agriculture in fish farming. We must trust the power and virtue of the advanced sciences and technology in providing new generations with high-quality food.

We must stop depleting the wild stocks, reducing our biodiversity and harming the oceans around us. Sustainable aquaculture, based on responsible modern biology, including genetic engineering, will provide the world with the seafood that we need and help conserve our planet.

Viewpoint 4

> *"Enviropig would eliminate the need for added phytase because the animal has been engineered to make its own."*

Genetically Engineered Pigs Could Provide Environmental Benefits

Anne Minard

In the following viewpoint, Anne Minard claims that researchers are working on a genetically engineered pig that could solve the problem of environmental damage caused by pig farming. Minard contends that the so-called Enviropig has been genetically modified with genes from other organisms to limit the amount of phosphorus that ends up in pig excrement. Minard claims that the Enviropig still faces hurdles in passing safety tests and proving a cost-benefit analysis for farmers. Minard is a science journalist.

As you read, consider the following questions:

1. According to the author, the Enviropig produces excrement with what percentage less phosphorus than non-engineered pigs?

2. The Enviropig is genetically modified with the genes of what bacterium, according to Minard?
3. According to Minard, the Food and Drug Administration (FDA) approved the first human health product made from a genetically engineered animal in what year?

Move over, bacon. Here comes something greener.

The Enviropig

A genetically engineered pig recently approved for limited production in Canada makes urine and feces that contain up to 65 percent less phosphorus, officials have announced.

That could be good news for lakes, rivers, and ocean deltas, where phosphorus from animal waste can play a role in causing algal blooms. These outbursts of algae rapidly deplete the water's oxygen, creating vast dead zones for fish and other aquatic life.

Dubbed Enviropig, the genetically altered animal cleared a major hurdle last month [February 2010], when the government-run Environment Canada approved the animal for production in controlled research settings.

The new biotech pig could take years to pass U.S. and Canadian tests for commercial use and human consumption, noted Steven Liss, an environmental scientist at the University of Guelph in Ontario and a spokesperson for the project.

But the Enviropig's creators are hopeful the animal will eventually pass muster.

"This will be probably the most significant transgenic food to be approved. We're in new territory," Liss said.

The Need for Genetically Engineered Food

The market may soon need Enviropig. To feed the projected world population of nine billion in 2050, food production will have to increase by 70 per cent, according to the Food and Agriculture Organization of the United Nations. Genetically engineered organisms will have to be part of the equation, according to the globe-spanning community of experts concerned with meeting those looming targets.

Jessica Leeder and Wency Leung,
"Canada's Transgenic Enviropig Is Stuck in a Genetic Modification Poke,"
Globe and Mail *(Canada), November 25, 2010.*

The Problem with Phosphorus

Like all living things, pigs need phosphorus from their food, because the element plays a key role in the formation of bones, teeth, and cell walls as well as in a variety of cellular and organ functions.

Swine in the United States primarily eat corn, while those in Canada munch on cereal grains, including barley. But the kind of phosphorus that occurs naturally in those plants is indigestible without an enzyme called phytase, which pigs lack.

Most farmers feed their pigs this enzyme as a supplement. But ingested phytase isn't as effective at breaking down phosphorus as phytase created inside the pig would be, so a fair amount of the element gets flushed out in pig waste. That waste, in turn, can make its way into the water supply.

Enviropig would eliminate the need for added phytase because the animal has been engineered to make its own.

A Genetic Modification

Researchers spent more than a decade hunting for an enzyme in nature responsible for breaking down phosphorus, finally finding it in the genome of the bacterium *E. coli.*

To make sure the modification would work in mammals, the team paired the *E. coli* genes with a mouse DNA promoter, a section of DNA that encourages replication of a specific segment—in this case the bacterial genes. Researchers then injected microscopic fertilized pig embryos with the mixture.

Early trials revealed that the bacterial enzyme was not only incorporated into the pig genome, it could be inherited by the genetically engineered pigs' offspring.

"We are now in the eighth generation of pigs, and it has been transmitted to all of those generations," said Cecil Forsberg, a University of Guelph microbiologist and lead researcher on the project.

"And from our testing, there is no change in the structure of the gene throughout those generations."

With the added genes, Enviropig is able to absorb more phosphorus from its feed, so less of the element ends up unused and excreted.

A Possible Benefit for Farmers

Enviropig addresses not only environmental concerns but also societal challenges in pig farming, the University of Guelph researchers say.

In addition to cutting feed-supplement costs, Enviropig could help farmers comply with "zero discharge" rules in the United States that allow no nitrogen or phosphorus runoff from animal operations.

Right now, most pork producers meet this law by collecting pig waste in pits and lagoons until it can be treated or recycled as fertilizer—resulting in added expenses for the farmers.

"The cost to produce animals is increasing, putting the burden on farmers in a global marketplace," project spokesperson Liss said.

Now that Enviropig has reached a milestone, pork producers will be watching to see if the transgenic animal passes safety tests with the U.S. Food and Drug Administration [FDA], noted Paul Sundberg, vice president of science and technology for the U.S. National Pork Board.

Industry professionals will also want to see a cost-benefit analysis, to be sure Enviropig will be a boon to the industry, Sundberg said.

"Pork producers are in favor of any technologies that can increase their competitiveness," he said.

So far, no transgenic animal has been approved for consumption in the United States. But in 2008 the FDA announced approval of the first human health product made from a genetically engineered animal.

The goat-derived anticoagulant, ATryn, is used for the prevention of blood clots in patients with a rare disease-causing protein deficiency.

VIEWPOINT 5

> *"Enviropig is a classic false technological fix that ignores the real causes of a problem."*

Genetically Engineered Pigs Are Not a Good Solution to Environmental Problems

Lucy Sharratt

In the following viewpoint, Lucy Sharratt argues that the development of a genetically engineered pig is not the fix for water pollution caused by factory farming. Sharratt claims that the real solution to the environmental damage of hog farming is smaller farms spaced further apart. She cautions that the safety of the so-called Enviropig has not been established, and she warns that allowing genetically modified pork in Canada could harm the hog farming industry. Sharratt is the coordinator of the Canadian Biotechnology Action Network.

As you read, consider the following questions:

1. Sharratt claims that excess phosphorus from pig farming causes environmental damage in what way?

Lucy Sharratt, "Enviropig: A Piggy You Hope Never to Meet at Market," *Common Ground–Canada*, no. 227, June 2010.

2. According to the author, the number of hog farms was cut by what fraction between 1996 and 2009?
3. Canada's hog producers exported to more than how many countries in 2009, according to Sharratt?

Fifteen years ago in a lab at the University of Guelph in Ontario—then home to some of Canada's most ardent supporters of the new science of genetic engineering—an idea was conceived. Five years later, "Wayne," a genetically modified (GM) pig was born. Now, the so-called "Enviropig" could soon be approved for human consumption in Canada and possibly the US as well.

A False Technological Fix

As technology grows increasingly complex and our environmental problems ever more serious, the proposed "technological fixes" from industry grow more ludicrous and dangerous. And so it is with genetic engineering. The common disconnect between science and reality is represented perfectly by the ridiculous, and yet threateningly real GM Enviropig project. Enviropig is the grotesque realization of early scientific aspirations and laboratory accidents. Born of scientific curiosity, hubris and a complete misunderstanding of the real world, a GM pig with less phosphorus in its feces is being proposed as a solution to water pollution caused by runoff from factory farms.

Enviropig is the trademarked industry name for a pig that has been genetically engineered to excrete less phosphorus in its feces. It will produce the enzyme phytase in its salivary glands to enable more effective digestion of phytate, the form of phosphorus found in pig feed ingredients like corn and soybeans. Scientists inserted a transgene sequence that includes an *E. coli* bacteria phytase gene and a mouse promoter gene sequence.

Enviropig is a classic false technological fix that ignores the real causes of a problem and instead tries to develop, at great cost, a shiny, new, patented product for sale to mask the symptoms.

The Problem with Phosphorus Pollution

Phosphorus from animal manure is a nutrient for plants that becomes a pollutant if there's too much of it for crops to absorb, and the excess runs off into streams and lakes. When pig manure spread on farmland exceeds the amount crops can use while growing, the excess phosphorus runs off as fields drain into surface waters. There, it promotes excessive algae growth. The algae form thick mats, blocking sunlight from reaching deeper waters and when the algae dies and decomposes, it uses up dissolved oxygen in the water, killing fish and other organisms. Blue-green algae, which often grow in phosphorus-rich waters, produce cyanotoxins that can kill livestock and pets if they drink the polluted water.

But phosphorus pollution is a problem specific to the industrial model of hog production where tens of thousands of pigs under one roof produce too much manure for the surrounding land to use productively. Such intensive, concentrated production means that operations import tonnes of pig feed from distant sources and must then pay the cost of disposing of millions of gallons of liquefied hog manure. Operations prefer to spread manure on land within a mile or two of the industrial pig barns rather than pay to transport heavy liquid manure to more distant fields.

Enviropig is designed to reduce the amount of phosphorus produced by the pigs themselves so factory farms don't have to pay for other measures, such as reducing the number of pigs they raise in one place, trucking liquid manure longer distances or expanding the area of land for spreading manure. The real solution, however, lies in changing the model of production, not in genetically engineering the pigs.

The Demise of Small Farms

Enviropig is expressly designed to support existing factory farming practices. In the early days, before the advent of extensive public relations, University of Guelph scientist and Enviropig developer John Philips said as much. In 1999, a Reuters article included Philips articulating the economic rationale that, if phosphorus in pig manure is reduced by 50 percent, theoretically, farmers can raise 50 percent more pigs and still meet environmental restrictions. Philips went on to say that, in North America, Europe and in some parts of Asia, the only thing holding back a farmer's hog output is the restriction on phosphorus leaching into the water table.

In an alternative model characterized by smaller hog production units dispersed over a wide geographic area, phosphorus in pig manure does not become an environmental problem; it is used as a valuable fertilizer instead. Phosphorus is an important plant nutrient and an essential element of soil fertility in farming. Animal manure is a source of phosphorus for growing field crops, including those used to feed pigs.

Twenty years ago, hog production in Canada was based on a successful model where tens of thousands of farmers earned a livelihood raising pigs in modest-sized operations. Now, the hog industry is dominated by a few giant hog production corporations where thousands of pigs are raised under one roof. Smaller, independent farmers have been forced out of business through loss of market access and unfair competition from huge, vertically integrated companies that own hog barns as well as packing plants and other related businesses. Hog production has doubled over the past 20 years, but in the 13 years between 1996 and 2009, the numbers of farms reporting hogs was cut by nearly two-thirds—from 21,105 to 7,675.

Canada's Hog Producers

Intensive production has made Canada a major global supplier of hogs, but we can't compete with other countries that have lower labour and feed costs. The result is that Canada's hog producers have been forced to sell below their cost of production for many years and small producers have retired, sold out or gone bankrupt. Only the biggest producers and some contract producers are left, surviving almost exclusively on government subsidy programs and bailout packages. Adding a GM pig to this economically and environmentally unsustainable model will only deepen the crisis.

Enviropig is the child of researchers at the University of Guelph and is almost fully funded by the public purse, with one exception. The hog producers' association, Ontario Pork, is the single private investor and has funded research and development to the tune of at least $1.371 million. The money invested came directly from Ontario hog producers who pay a compulsory fee to the association on each hog marketed in Ontario. Ontario Pork holds an exclusive licence to distribute the pig to swine breeders and producers worldwide, but the association might want to rethink this plan in light of the global uproar over GM pork it is about to witness.

What might have looked like a progressive and technologically advanced position 10 years ago has been overtaken by other technological developments, namely an enzyme feed supplement that can cut phosphorus by around 30 percent.

The Safety of Enviropig

Enviropig, like all GM foods in Canada, will be assessed for human safety by Health Canada and classified as a "novel food." Health Canada, however, has not yet developed specific guidelines for evaluating the safety of GM animals for human consumption. Instead, Canada will rely on the United Nations Codex [Alimentarius] guidelines and refer to the US Food and Drug Administration. Health Canada does not conduct any of its own safety tests of GM foods, but relies on data submitted directly from the product developer, in this case the University of Guelph. The data is classified as "Confidential

Business Information" and is not accessible to the public or to independent scientists. Of course, there is no mandatory labelling of GM foods in Canada or the US so approval of GM pork is likely to spark an unprecedented crisis of consumer confidence in the food system.

We have already witnessed the biosafety risk posed by Enviropig. In 2002, a precedent for contamination of the food system by Enviropig was set when eleven GM piglets at the university were sent to a rendering plant and turned into animal feed instead of being destroyed as biological waste. The GM pigs were not approved for animal feed and they contaminated 675 tonnes of poultry feed that was sold to egg farmers, turkey farmers and broiler chicken producers in Ontario. As then vice president of research at the University of Guelph told the *Globe and Mail*, "Things you don't expect to happen can happen."

That incident was not the only time that experimental GM pigs have contaminated the food system in Canada. In 2004, experimental GM pharma-pigs from the Quebec company TGN Biotech were accidentally turned into chicken feed instead of being incinerated. . . .

A Bad Choice for Canada

Canada's hog producers rely on export sales more than any other country, exporting to more than 110 countries in 2009. But the predictable scenario is worldwide rejection of GM pork, causing harm to Canadian export sales and depressing prices.

The reality is that hog farming in Canada is already in deep economic crisis. For several years, farmers have been losing money on every hog they sell, surviving primarily on off-farm jobs and government subsidies. While managing phosphorus overproduction is a cost for intensive operations, the GM pig will likely also come at a very high price. Patented

GM technologies are notoriously expensive and control over them is wielded to bleed farmers of as much money as possible.

With so many large-scale industrial hog operations collapsing in Canada, a return to smaller, less concentrated hog production—combined with other policies that ensure independent farmers have access to markets, get a fair share of returns, and are not undercut by cheap imports from jurisdictions with weak environmental and labour laws—could also be the solution to the severe income crisis in the hog industry.

Enviropig was allowed to happen because there has never been a democratic debate in Canada about genetic engineering and there is no public overview of the direction of public research. Not only did Canadians pay for the research and development of Enviropig, we are now paying for Health Canada to decide if it's safe enough for us to eat.

Periodical and Internet Sources Bibliography

The following articles have been selected to supplement the diverse views presented in this chapter.

Willy De Greef	"GM Food for Thought," *European Voice*, November 19, 2009.
Jon Entine	"GM Salmon: Take a Leap of Faith," *Ethical Corporation*, September 2010.
Food & Water Watch	"Below the Surface: The Dangers of Genetically Engineered Salmon," Fact Sheet, June 2011.
Food & Water Watch	"'Enviropig' or FrankenSwine? Why Genetically Modifying Pigs Could Cause a Load of Manure," Fact Sheet, June 2010.
James Greenwood	"Genetically Engineered Fish Is Answer to Seafood Crisis," *Natural Resource Report*, October 3, 2010.
Matthew Herper	"Green Genes: Are Genetically Modified Crops Eco-Friendly?," *Forbes*, March 1, 2010.
Robin McKie	"Why the Case for GM Salmon Is Still Hard to Stomach," *Guardian* (United Kingdom), August 27, 2010.
Josh Ozersky	"How I Learned to Love Farmed Fish," *Time*, September 1, 2010.
Tom Philpott	"Wait, Did the USDA Just Deregulate All New Genetically Modified Crops?," *Mother Jones*, July 8, 2011.
Heather Rogers	"Against the Grain," *Washington Monthly*, November/December 2010.

OPPOSING VIEWPOINTS® SERIES

CHAPTER 4

How Should Genetic Engineering Technology Be Regulated?

Chapter Preface

Scientific advancement has made genetic engineering possible. Just because science has made this technology possible, however, does not mean that scientists are proceeding unfettered. Much debate exists about how the use of genetic engineering technology should be regulated. One of the early battles over regulation of a particular use of genetic modification illustrates some of the common issues surrounding the oversight of genetic technologies.

Dairy farmers have used bovine somatotropin to increase milk production in dairy cows since the 1930s, but the use of this hormone was limited since the only source of this hormone, which occurs naturally in cows, was from cow cadavers. In 1993 the US Food and Drug Administration (FDA) approved the use of a genetically modified hormone—recombinant bovine somatotropin, or rBST—and many dairy farmers began using the hormone to increase the milk production of their cows by 10 to 25 percent. According to the FDA, no significant difference has been shown in milk from rBST-treated cows and untreated cows.

The use of rBST is banned in Canada, all countries of the European Union, Japan, Australia, and New Zealand. Among the reasons for the ban in these countries are concerns about animal welfare and concerns about human health. The European Commission's Scientific Committee on Animal Health and Animal Welfare (SCAHAW) concluded in 1999 that the use of rBST posed a problem for animal welfare.

> BST use causes a substantial increase in levels of foot problems and mastitis and leads to injection site reactions in dairy cows. These conditions, especially the first two, are painful and debilitating, leading to significantly poorer welfare in the treated animals. Therefore from the point of view of animal welfare, including health, the Scientific Committee

> on Animal Health and Animal Welfare is of the opinion that BST should not be used in cows.[1]

SCAHAW's report was cited in the European Commission's 1999 decision to ban the use of rBST in the European Union. Although impact on human health was not cited as a reason for the ban, concerns had been raised by the European Commission's Scientific Committee on Veterinary Measures Relating to Public Health (SCVPH) about the possible health dangers to humans from the increased concentration of insulin-like growth factor 1 (IGF-1) in milk from cows treated with rBST.

In the United States, controversy over the use of rBST has centered on labeling of milk from cows treated with rBST, since the FDA does not require labeling of such milk. Monsanto, the company that makes the most popular rBST product, sued Oakhurst Dairy of Maine in 2003 over a label on their milk stating, "Our Farmers' Pledge: No Artificial Hormones." The lawsuit was settled out of court and Oakhurst Dairy agreed to add the statement, "FDA states: No significant difference in milk from cows treated with artificial growth hormones." Across the country, dairy farmers who do not use rBST have followed suit, labeling the milk as such, but with the FDA disclaimer. Thus, although the FDA does not require milk produced with rBST to be labeled, milk produced without it is frequently labeled as such by the farmers.

Public opinion of rBST has been mixed. Opposition to the use of the hormone caused Walmart, Safeway, and Starbucks to decide not to carry milk from cows treated with rBST, causing a drop in use of the genetically modified hormone. A 2010 Thomson Reuters poll found that 93 percent of Americans want genetically modified foods labeled. Thus, whether they are willing to consume genetically modified food or not, public opinion about labeling is fairly clear. Nonetheless, the

1. Scientific Committee on Animal Health and Animal Welfare (SCAHAW), "Report on Animal Welfare Aspects of the Use of Bovine Somatotropin," 1999.

FDA continues to claim that there is no difference between milk from cows treated with rBST and other milk, thus standing by its decision that labeling is not required. Public controversy about the safety of genetically modified foods and the need for labeling of such foods does not show any sign of abating in the near future.

Viewpoint 1

> *"Putting our trust in commercial markets and the free play of human desire would unleash a genetic enhancement rat race that could never be contained."*

New Genetic Engineering Technology Needs to Be Regulated

Richard Hayes

In the following viewpoint, Richard Hayes argues that despite the challenges in delineating acceptable from unacceptable uses of human genetic technologies, national and international policies are necessary to prevent such technologies from having a negative impact. Hayes is executive director of the Center for Genetics and Society, an organization working to encourage responsible uses and effective societal governance of new human genetic and reproductive technologies.

As you read, consider the following questions:

1. What example does Hayes use to describe a gray area where a particular genetic technology can be used for both therapeutic and cosmetic purposes?

Richard Hayes, "Is There an Emerging International Consensus on the Proper Uses of the New Human Genetic Technologies?," Testimony Before the House Foreign Affairs Committee, Subcommittee on Terrorism, Nonproliferation, and Trade, June 19, 2008, pp. 8–10.

2. The author claims that what problem would result from a ban on reproductive cloning in only some of the world's countries?
3. What two reasons does Hayes give to explain the fact that Europe has some of the strictest regulations over human genetic technology?

The new human genetic technologies are a case study of what economists, political scientists and game theoreticians call the *prisoner's dilemma* or the *collective action problem*, and what environmentalists have called the *tragedy of the commons*. Situations frequently arise in which the choices any of us might make as individuals, can, if chosen by everyone, generate negative consequences that everyone regrets.

The Challenges of New Genetic Technologies

A parent might fantasize that it would be gratifying to have a child who is an athletic superstar, perhaps through genetic enhancement, but on reflection conclude that they would not want their child to live in a world in which such genetic enhancement, building at a constantly accelerating pace, had become the norm. If enough parents shared this concern, they could collectively agree to forego the possibility of genetic enhancement. In large societies such agreements are codified and enforced through laws and regulations. Indeed, the existence of such collective action problems is the reason that governments exist in the first place. There is no inherent reason to expect that democratic governments will not be able to address collective action problems posed by the new human genetic technologies.

It's true, however, that these technologies pose special challenges. They are very new, and neither the general public nor policy makers have had the occasion to fully consider what is happening and what is at stake. The trade-offs between acceptable and unacceptable uses are clear in many instances but not in others, and people are understandably reluctant to forego possible benefits without good reason. . . .

Some applications of genetic technology fall into definitional gray areas. If it were possible to use germ-line engineering to create a child with immunity to all major diseases, would this constitute "therapy" or "enhancement?" Using genetic technology to allow a child lacking a key growth hormone gene to grow to normal height might be considered therapeutic, but what about allowing children with normal hormone functioning, but who are nonetheless very short, to use genetic technology to similarly grow to normal height?

The Need to Draw Lines

Some have argued that the fact that it is difficult to draw bright lines regarding the therapy/enhancement distinction means that no lines *can* be drawn. But this is a specious argument. Public policy is in large part a matter of drawing lines; we do it all the time. Putting our trust in commercial markets and the free play of human desire would unleash a genetic enhancement rat race that could never be contained. The responsible alternative is to establish as a matter of law the clearest lines possible and a clear statement of intent, and delegate decisions over remaining gray areas—which typically impact fewer individuals—to accountable regulatory bodies. Such structures have been put in place in the United Kingdom, Canada, France and many other countries. . . .

Another challenge is the fact that some policies will need to be universal, or nearly so, if they are to be meaningful at all. It does little good if the great majority of the world's countries agree to ban human reproductive cloning while a handful decide to distinguish themselves as free havens for the creation of human clones. If these countries are small this may be a small problem and resolvable through diplomacy, but if they are large this would be a large problem. In this regard, it is worth noting that neither Russia nor the United States has yet banned human reproductive cloning.

We also need to acknowledge that in a world still far from having overcome our readiness to resort to xenophobia and armed conflict, the possibility of a techno-eugenic arms race driven by nationalist fervor cannot be dismissed. In 2000 concern about massively lethal applications motivated computer scientist Bill Joy to call for a permanent halt to particular avenues of genetic research. In 2003 the Sunshine Project documented nearly a dozen possible uses of genetic science for biowarfare purposes, including the creation of ethnicity-specific pathogens. In November 2006 Kofi Annan, in one of his final addresses as UN [United Nations] secretary-general, urgently called for new international treaties guarding against the development and use of genetically enhanced bioweapons. We have been moderately—but only moderately—successfully in containing the spread of nuclear, chemical and conventional biological weapons. We now need to add bioweaponry incorporating human genetic technology to our arms control portfolio.

Moving Beyond the Culture Wars

Given the stark nature of the potential threats posed by the new human genetic technologies, why has more attention not been paid to addressing them? One reason is that in many countries, including the United States, the debate over policy concerning the new human biotechnologies has become enmeshed in the political dynamics of the culture wars. Religious conservatives were the first to become vocal on high-profile issues such as human cloning, and the debate over the new human genetic technologies was quickly framed within the conventional categories of abortion politics. In response, many liberals assumed that the progressive response was therefore one of largely uncritical support. The result has been a stalemate and a policy vacuum at the federal level and hastily

Policies Worldwide on Genetic Technologies (192 Countries)

	Number of countries in which the practice is explicitly:	
Practice	**Allowed**	**Prohibited**
Medically related trait selection	30	6
Embryonic SCR (Stem Cell Research) using IVF (In Vitro Fertilization) embryos	44	12
Social trait selection	0	36
Research cloning	14	40
Germ line modification	0	44
Reproductive cloning	0	59

TAKEN FROM: Richard Hayes, "Is There an Emerging International Consensus on the Proper Uses of the New Human Genetic Technologies?," Testimony Before the House Foreign Affairs Committee, Subcommittee on Terrorism, Nonproliferation, and Trade, June 19, 2008.

conceived human biotechnology funding programs at the state levels. At the international level, the result has been avoidance and neglect.

However, opinion surveys repeatedly show broad support for what might be called a principled middle-ground position concerning the new human genetic technologies. The majority of people—in America and much of the rest of the world—do not necessarily oppose all research involving human embryos, but they strongly reject reproductive cloning and the engineering or selecting of the social traits of future generations.

The issues raised by the new human genetic technologies transcend conventional ideological divides. Many pro-choice women's health advocates oppose new genetic and reproductive technologies that put women's health and well-being at risk and raise concerns about the commodification of reproduction and human relationships. Human and civil rights leaders are wary of a new free-market eugenics that could stoke the fires of racial and ethnic hatred. Disability rights leaders charge that a society obsessed with genetic perfection could come to regard the disabled as mistakes that should have been prevented. Many environmentalists see human genetic modification as another hubristic technology being promoted with little regard for long-range consequences.

It is likewise misleading to use the conventional categories of "left/right" or "liberal/conservative" to categorize the responses of different countries to human biotechnology concerns. Western European countries widely regarded as bastions of secular liberalism have adopted some of the strictest regulations over human genetic technology in the world. This derives from their generally social democratic political culture, and from their firsthand experience in the 20th century with eugenics, euthanasia and the Holocaust. Europeans know all too well what can happen when ideologies and policies that valorize the creation of "genetically superior" human beings come to the fore. For different but related reasons, developing countries such as South Africa, Vietnam, India and Brazil have likewise adopted policies of social oversight and control.

Despite many statements to the contrary, the genie is *not* out of the bottle. In any event, some of the genies are *good* genies, and the *worst* genies are still *in* the bottle. I sincerely believe we have the time and the capability to get ahead of the curve and do the right thing. But it will require committed engagement on the part of social and political leaders, socially responsible scientists, representatives of the world's major religious traditions, opinion leaders, public intellectuals and the press, and, finally, the general public, if we are to adopt responsible policies ensuring that the new human genetic technologies are used to improve the human condition rather than jeopardize it.

Viewpoint 2

"What [Professor Francis] Fukuyama is proposing is a step backward to the bad old days in which strangers get to vote on what kind of children their fellow citizens will be allowed to bring into the world."

New Genetic Engineering Technology Does Not Need to Be Regulated

Ronald Bailey

In the following viewpoint, Ronald Bailey argues that proposed regulation of human reproductive biotechnology is unnecessary and dangerous. Bailey claims that the impact of the United Kingdom's biotechnology regulatory agency and the historical experience of the United States with government regulation of human reproduction speak against the development of any new regulatory agency. Bailey concludes that the moral thing to do is to not meddle in people's reproductive decisions. Bailey is science correspondent for Reason *and author of* Liberation Biology: The Scientific and Moral Case for the Biotech Revolution.

Ronald Bailey, "Medievalizing Biotech Regulation," Reason.com, March 9, 2007. Reproduced by permission.

As you read, consider the following questions:

1. The proposal for the new biotech regulatory agency that the author opposes is modeled after what foreign agency?
2. According to Bailey, what five biotechnologies does Francis Fukuyama propose banning completely?
3. What four US Supreme Court decisions does the author cite as reversing state laws that interfered with the reproductive decisions of Americans?

"We are proposing a new regulatory institution in Washington, DC," said Francis Fukuyama, professor of political economy at the Johns Hopkins University [Paul H. Nitze] School of Advanced International Studies and author of *Our Posthuman Future*. "It's been a long time since anyone has done that."

Regulation for Human Biotechnology

What needs regulating? Human biotechnology. Fukuyama unveiled his plan for a new agency at a conference held at the Rayburn House Office Building on Capitol Hill. The blueprint for the new biotech regulatory agency being proposed by Fukuyama and Swiss technology consultant Franco Furger is laid out in a 400-page book, *Beyond Bioethics: A Proposal for Modernizing the Regulation of Human Biotechnologies.*

Why do we need a new biotech regulatory agency? Because bad things have happened? Not at all. In fact, Fukuyama wants to put his proposal in play now so that the denizens of Capitol Hill can simply pull it off the shelf and enact it into law when some sort of biotech scandal erupts. The proposed agency is explicitly modeled after the British Human Fertilisation and Embryology Authority (HFEA). Fukuyama's new agency would not just regulate the safety and efficacy of new biotechnologies, but also rule on their ethical propriety. According to Fukuyama, biotechnology is "galloping ahead" and it's time to move from ethical discussions to regulation and "social control."

Furger discussed some recent developments to illustrate how biotech is galloping ahead. For example, a Texas fertility clinic is now offering embryos for sale; researchers have manufactured mouse sperm from stem cells; and others have inserted human cell nuclei into rabbit eggs to try to produce stem cells. Furger said that he was listing these activities "not to say that they are reproachable. Some may be acceptable and some not." He asked, "But how do we make that determination?"

The Proposal for a New Agency

Fukuyama explained that the new agency would regulate anything having to do with assisted reproduction techniques (ART). This would include IVF [in vitro fertilization], ooplasm transfer, sex selection either by preimplantation genetic diagnosis (PGD) or sperm sorting. The agency would also regulate research involving human reproductive tissues including all embryonic stem cell research and anything dealing with human developmental biology.

"Biotech has reached a point where existing regulators, the Food and Drug Administration and the National Institutes of Health, can't handle it," declared Fukuyama. The agency would be guided by a set of ranked ethical principles. Its first concern would be the well-being and health of children. Second, ensuring equal access to ART for infertile couples. Third, protecting the well-being of and health of women. Fourth, promoting therapeutic uses of ART over enhancement uses. Fifth, making sure that patients and research subjects give their free informed consent to procedures. And finally, advocating for regulations to limit the commercialization of human eggs, sperm and embryos.

Fukuyama would completely ban human reproductive cloning, the creation of human animal chimeras for the purpose of reproduction, germ-line genetic modifications, any procedure that would alter the genetic relationship of parents to children, and the patenting of human embryos.

The new agency would regulate research cloning, PGD, sex selection of embryos, and the commercialization of certain elements of human reproduction such as the sale of eggs, sperm and embryos. It would consist of a set of commissioners, appointed by the president and advised by a board consisting of various stakeholder groups such as patients, ART practitioners, [and members of the] scientific community and the biotech industry. Fukuyama also introduced a novel set of mechanisms for consulting with the wider public including deliberative panels and a consultative college consisting of randomly selected members of the public who convene to consider regulatory issues over the Internet.

The Dangers of Government Regulation

Instead of inhibiting research and the development of new treatments, the new agency could spur them on, suggested Fukuyama. For example, he asserted that Britain is ahead of the United States in human embryonic stem cell research because of the HFEA's regulations. Fukuyama is just plain wrong about that. The *Guardian* reported last week [March 2, 2007], "Excessive bureaucracy imposed by the Human Fertilisation and Embryology Authority [is] prohibiting development in stem cell research and threatening Britain's position as a world leader in the field." The *Guardian* quoted stem cell researcher Alison Murdoch, director of the Newcastle [Fertility] Centre [at] Life fertility clinic, as saying, "The way the government has handled the work we do is to regulate it to the point that it looks like it's got barbed wire around it."

But what about the larger question: Do we really want a federal agency making and imposing ethical decisions about

The Proposed Biotechnology Regulation

Activities we believe are ethically legitimate, but ought to be carried out under carefully controlled circumstances, include:

Research cloning. We believe that research cloning should be permitted but tightly regulated. We see why many people who are not troubled by the use of excess embryos in stem cell research may yet oppose the deliberate creation of cloned embryos for research purposes. We believe, however, that whatever extra instrumentalization this act may imply does not outweigh the gains potentially to be derived from this kind of research. It is, however, particularly important for the regulatory authority to monitor and control this kind of research very carefully—not just because of what we call the intermediate moral status of embryos, but also because it is the only way to enforce a ban on reproductive cloning.

Preimplantation genetic diagnosis. Preimplantation genetic diagnosis (PGD) is a service performed by many fertility clinics. We believe it is an important way for couples with heritable genetic disorders to ensure that those conditions are not passed down to their children. On the other hand, PGD involves certain kinds of risks and creates incentives . . . that could pose serious health problems for the women involved. Using PGD for nontherapeutic purposes raises a host of ethical issues, and should be strongly discouraged by the regulatory system.

Francis Fukuyama and Franco Furger,
Beyond Bioethics: A Proposal for Modernizing the Regulation of Human Biotechnologies.
Washington, DC: Paul H. Nitze School of Advanced International Studies, 2006, p. 6.

human reproduction? Consider the wretched history of federal and state regulation in this area. In 1873, Congress passed the Comstock Laws that outlawed "every obscene, lewd, or lascivious, and every filthy book, pamphlet, picture, paper, letter, writing, print, or other publication of an indecent character, and every article or thing designed, adapted, or intended for preventing conception or producing abortion." The Comstock Laws authorized the U.S. Post Office to confiscate any publications providing advice on contraception and condoms shipped through the mail. The first eugenics law was passed in Indiana in 1907 and eventually laws allowing the forced sterilization of "unfit" people were adopted by 30 states. Infamously, the U.S. Supreme Court upheld forced sterilization in the case of *Buck v. Bell* in 1927. By the 1960s, some 66,000 Americans had been forcibly neutered.

In the last half of the 20th century, the U.S. Supreme Court finally stepped in to overrule state interference in the reproductive decisions of Americans. In 1965, the court found unconstitutional the Connecticut law prohibiting use of birth control by married couples in *Griswold v. Connecticut*. In 1967, the court ruled in *Loving v. Virginia* that the laws in 16 states banning interracial marriage were unconstitutional. In 1972, the court struck down in the case of *Eisenstadt v. Baird* a Massachusetts law prohibiting the sale of contraceptives to unmarried people. And of course, the Supreme Court found prohibitions on abortion unconstitutional in 1973 in *Roe v. Wade*.

The Moral Thing to Do

The HFEA, the model for Fukuyama's new biotech regulatory agency, has similarly interfered with the reproductive decisions of British people. The HFEA has told couples that they could not select the sex of embryos to be implanted. Even now the parents wanting to use PGD to insure that their children will not be burdened with an inherited genetic disease must apply for permission from the HFEA. And the HFEA has banned paying women for providing eggs to be used in research.

Fukuyama's agency would rule not only on safety and efficacy but on moral questions surrounding human reproduction. Some possible techniques are objectionable and should be banned, e.g., any attempt to create a half-human half-chimp baby. On the other hand, Fukuyama wants to ban ever allowing parents to safely choose genes that would tend to give their children healthier immune systems, stronger bodies and cleverer brains.

It turns out that the proposed agency is largely just a vehicle for Fukuyama to impose his moral choices on other people. What Fukuyama is proposing is a step backward to the bad old days in which strangers get to vote on what kind of children their fellow citizens will be allowed to bring into the world. A government bureaucracy, rather than parents, would get to make eugenic decisions. As the sorry history of attempts to regulate human reproduction shows, the truly moral thing to do is fiercely resist this proposal.

VIEWPOINT 3

> *"The steps needed to protect the public have been clearly laid out by the various public interest groups and advisory panels."*

Knowing Me, Knowing You

Jeanne Lenzer and Shannon Brownlee

In the following viewpoint, Jeanne Lenzer and Shannon Brownlee contend that the direct-to-consumer genetic testing industry is growing rapidly in a regulatory vacuum, leading to the potential for harm to the consumers who use the tests. Lenzer and Brownlee claim that the potential harms to the consumer, including misinformation about disease potential and the risk of future discrimination, need to be addressed by regulation. Lenzer is a medical investigative journalist in New York and Brownlee is acting director of the New America Foundation's Health Policy Program.

As you read, consider the following questions:

1. According to the authors, the global direct-to-consumer genetic testing market is growing by what percentage annually?

Jeanne Lenzer and Shannon Brownlee, "Knowing Me, Knowing You," *BMJ*, vol. 336, no. 7649, April 19, 2008, pp. 858–860. Reproduced by permission.

2. Why is widespread genetic testing more likely to result in anxiety than in improved health, according to Lenzer and Brownlee?

3. Despite potential benefits, the authors caution that genomic databases have raised what concern?

Patients are beginning to present with not only a web diagnosis but predictions of future disease. Jeanne Lenzer and Shannon Brownlee examine the problems of the rise in commercial genetic testing.

Do you want to Google your genes or peer into your future risks of heart disease or cancer? Now you can, according to direct to consumer testing companies. Gone are the days when genetic testing was limited to doctors ordering tests for rare, but prognostically potent, single gene disorders such as Huntington's disease, Duchenne muscular dystrophy, or cystic fibrosis. Thanks to an explosion of newly discovered single nucleotide polymorphisms, or SNPs (pronounced snips), companies are marketing genetic tests for traits ranging from the mundane—eye colour and wet ear wax—to serious conditions such as Crohn's disease and Alzheimer's disease.

While the global market for these tests is growing rapidly—estimated at $730m (£366m; €463m) last year and growing by 20% annually[1]—evidence that they can provide patients with clinically useful information is lagging far behind. There is little regulatory oversight of the tests, and even less in the way of clinical data to help doctors guide patients who go to them carrying printouts of their genetic details. Genetic tests and "personalised medicine" are supposed to enable doctors to customise each patient's care, yet there is a paucity of studies on interventions for patients with genetic variants.

The promise being made to consumers is clear: forewarned is forearmed. The website for deCODE genetics, based in Reykjavik, says its tests will "help to empower individuals and their doctors." The Californian company 23andMe, which has backing from Google and the biotech company Genentech, provides an "odds calculator" that the company says will allow customers to see which "health concerns are most likely to affect a person with your genetic profile." Navigenics, also based in California, claims its tests can provide a "road map to optimal health" that can enable customers to "take action before a disorder strikes to delay or even prevent the illness altogether." And all for a fee ranging from $1000 to $2500.

A more likely scenario is that these tests will raise more questions than they answer. It is unclear what consumers think they are learning from their "genetic blueprints." Some screening tests, though noninvasive and seemingly harmless, have been shown to trigger a cascade of further evaluations and interventions that result in measurable harms while providing no benefit.[2-5]

Although widespread genetic testing might eventually lead to well-defined risk profiles and the ability to tailor drugs to the individual, such results may not be available for many years. In the meantime, genetic testing poses important and largely unacknowledged risks. As well as clinical concerns, there are questions about the effect of the corporate partnerships that link genomic data-mining companies to electronic medical records, hospitals, and drug companies.

Genomics Revolution

Direct to consumer genetic testing has its roots in the Human Genome Project, which was launched in 1984 with the promise of opening frontiers in medicine. Novel, personalised treatments would flow from an understanding of genetic underpinnings of disease, and some experts predict that the genomics revolution is poised to deliver information that will allow people to make personalised lifestyle changes or decide whether to have a child, and allow doctors to prescribe correct drugs at correct doses.[6] Linda Avey, cofounder of 23andMe, is an advocate of personalised medicine. "We're still using very antiquated systems for diagnosis and for prescribing therapies. Whenever you take a drug it's kind of a gamble whether your body will respond appropriately to it," she said.

Thus far, however, only a handful of genetic tests can indicate how a patient will react to a drug, and even then, the test may lack clinical value. For example, a working group that reviewed studies of dosing of serotonin reuptake inhibitor drugs based on the CYP450 polymorphism concluded that there is no evidence that the test is "useful in medical, personal, or public health decision making."[7] Even the discovery of the genes for many single gene conditions has failed to lead to the expected cures. For some diseases, like Huntington's disease and sickle-cell anaemia, the prospects for treatment seem as remote as they were before the genes were discovered.

Along with genetic information, some companies offer to calculate a customer's risk of developing conditions such as type 2 diabetes, cardiovascular disease, and prostate and breast cancer. 23andMe, for example, offers a scan of some 580,000 SNPs and a report on roughly 14 conditions for which customers might be at risk. These risk calculations are exceedingly rough, however, as most SNPs have been only loosely connected to any particular disease, and there are few hard numbers that can accurately predict the contribution of a particular polymorphism to an individual's phenotypic risk.

A lack of data has not stopped genomics companies from capitalising on the appealing concept of personalised medicine, starting with their names, which include 23andMe (23 chromosomes), deCODEme, and Knome (pronounced know me). Knome is founded by George Church, professor of genetics at Harvard, who helped develop the first direct genomic sequencing method. For upwards of $350,000, Knome will sequence a customer's entire genome. 23andMe also provides genetic information for "entertainment" and "education" purposes, such as whether one has generic markers for an enhanced ability to taste bitterness or for athleticism.

Companies are careful to acknowledge in the fine print the lack of meaningful data. In a special message "To the Medical Community," 23andMe acknowledges that the information it provides "is tailored to genotypes not to individuals"—an acknowledgment that belies the claim of personalised, clinically relevant health information. But 23andMe cofounder Anne Wojcicki argues that people have a right to know their genetic information and says that the company is not providing "actionable" health information but information that is largely intended to educate and lead to better research.

But what is it that customers are being educated about? When asked if customers of 23andMe were under the impression that they could obtain health information that would be useful to them, Professor Church, who is an adviser to 23andMe, responded, "I hope not." He added, "Education is useful, but distinct from clinically accepted diagnoses."

Estimating Risk

Nevertheless, doctors are likely to be seeing more and more patients arriving at their doors, genomic results in hand, requesting treatment for diseases they do not yet have or more screening tests. Most doctors, according to a recent systematic review by RAND Health, are "woefully underprepared" to counsel patients about genetic tests.[8] According to one study cited in the review, only 5% of doctors said they felt "confident in their ability to interpret test results."

Rather than improving health, widespread genetic testing is likely to result in widespread anxiety. In a commentary published in *JAMA*, Gilbert Welch and Wylie Burke caution that there is substantial confusion about estimates of genetic risk.[9] Selection bias, they say, can lead to "overestimates of both risks and consequences of disease." For example, the oft cited 87% risk of cancer by the age of 70 years among women who test positive for the BRCA1 gene was derived from tests of exceptionally high-risk women who had at least four family members with ovarian or breast cancer diagnosed before age 60 years. Far lower estimates were obtained when the inclusion criteria for testing were broadened.[9] Another form of bias, surveillance bias, can lead to similar exaggeration of risk when people with a certain genetic trait choose to have more frequent testing. "The quickest way to develop breast cancer," said Dr Welch, "is to be tested for it."

Framing risk can have a powerful effect—an effect that genomics companies are putting to use when marketing their tests. The website of 23andMe warns of a "1 in 8" chance of developing breast cancer, a risk that can be expected to alarm many women. Yet a woman's risk is that high only once she reaches the age of 70. In the US, such risk estimates have led many women to overestimate their chances of dying of breast cancer, which accounts for only 3% of female deaths annually.[10]

Similarly, telling men (accurately) that more than half of them will have prostate cancer by the age of 60 years, and that men with certain genetic variants have a four times greater risk of developing prostate cancer than men with none of those variants (also accurate) could understandably persuade some men to have prostate specific antigen testing.[10] But if the information is framed differently, men might not be so enthusiastic. "Only 3% of men die of prostate cancer," Dr Welch says. Instead of telling men that they are at an 80% increased risk of developing prostate cancer, he says, doctors should tell men that their lifetime risk of dying from prostate cancer is 3%. "And an 80% increase of that risk doesn't even increase the risk to 6%."

Research Benefits

The potential payoff, for both patients and companies, lies with pharmacogenomics, the development of new, more personalised drugs. This requires access to huge numbers of research subjects, their genomes, and their phenotypic (clinical) records—an extraordinarily expensive undertaking. In a clever reversal, companies are getting research subjects to pay—rather than be paid—to become research subjects. Genetic testing companies' primary source of income is fees paid by customers. In the future, they can expect to earn even more by selling the genomic information they gather to researchers and to biotechnology and drug companies. Customers of 23andMe sign a consent document indicating that the company may share their genomic data (anonymously) and that the company may sell the data to researchers. Customers of 23andMe are asked if they would like to make their health records available (free) to researchers to advance medical science.

Companies are planning ways to integrate genomic data with phenotypic information from patients' electronic records. Google, which invested $3.9m in 23andMe, is poised to launch its online personal health records. (The cofounder of Google, Sergey Brin, is married to Anne Wojcicki, cofounder of 23andMe.) Ms Avey says 23andMe plans to work with personal health record companies to enable data merger.

Although 23andMe insists it is in the business of advancing research, its commercial appeal to the public suggests a different interest. Dr Welch says that telling customers about their risk factors could result in surveillance bias. "They might be conducting research," he said, "but it won't be good research."

The potential gold mine in combining genomic and phenotypic information is evident from the fact that at least one company, the Coriell Institute for Medical Research in New Jersey, is offering genetic testing to 10,000 people. The institute has partnered with several health care organisations, including Cooper University Hospital, which is offering Coriell's free genomic screening to the first 2000 of its 5500 employees who sign up. The response has been "overwhelmingly positive," according to a hospital spokeswoman. Cooper's chief medical officer, Simon Samaha, says that the hospital is planning training sessions for doctors, who expect an influx of patients after the screening.

While genomic databases may lead to better drugs, integrating genomic and phenotypic data has raised concerns about potential discrimination by insurance companies and employers. In the US, antidiscrimination laws vary from state to state, and there is little agreement among payers, physicians, researchers, and patients about whether insurance companies should have access to genomic information. Dr Samaha says that he's not sure that it's wrong for insurance companies to have access to such genomic data: "It raises a question about how open the economy should be."

Failed Regulation

Concerned with the potential for harm, advisory bodies in the US and UK have recommended regulatory oversight of direct to consumer genetic testing—yet national agencies in both countries have failed to act. According to Public Citizen's Health Research Group, a public interest group based in Washington, DC, the 2004 draft report by the US Secretary's Advisory Committee on Genetics, Health and Society was "notable" for its "accurate diagnosis of the manifold problems in the oversight of genetic testing and . . . for its complete failure to identify an appropriate treatment for these problems."[11]

Critics say that regulatory oversight is uneven to nonexistent. There is little oversight of clinical validity (is the genetic variant reliably associated with the phenotypic change observed?) and clinical utility (do enhanced surveillance, prophylactic treatment, or lifestyle changes improve outcome?).

Even accurate detection of genetic variants is not necessarily assured. In 1997 and 2001, US governmental groups and an earlier advisory panel recommended proficiency testing for all laboratories doing genetic tests—but those recommendations were simply ignored by federal agencies.[12] In an almost comical response, the Centers for Medicare and Medicaid Services, the agency responsible for ensuring analytical validity under the Clinical Laboratory Improvement Amendments, argued that setting laboratory standards for genetic testing was too difficult. To prove its point, it cited the agency's previous difficulty in ensuring the accuracy of cervical smear testing, which took 17 years to complete. The reason the amendments were passed (and proficiency testing instituted) was because of massive malpractice suits resulting from the deaths of women whose cervical smears had been misread.[12]

Peter Lurie, deputy director of Public Citizen's Health Research Group, is disturbed by the lack of oversight of genetic testing. He worries that the public may "assume there is the same degree of oversight" for genetic tests as there is for tests such as a red blood cell count. "But," he said, "they are not even remotely the same." Similar problems plague the UK. Sir John Sulston, acting chair of the Human Genetics Commission, which lacks regulatory authority, says that nothing has changed since December 2007, when he wrote that direct to consumer genetic testing is "for now, largely in the hands of commercial test providers: the pharmaceutical companies, their marketing departments and PR agents."[13]

What all this means is that testing companies are operating in a regulatory vacuum. The steps needed to protect the public have been clearly laid out by the various public interest groups and advisory panels. Until national agencies act, it will be up to doctors to handle the expected influx of questions and problems that arise from direct to consumer genetic testing. The first step towards reducing the chances of harm posed by widespread genetic testing is to educate doctors and patients about the limited value and potential harms of testing.[11-13]

Perhaps the most powerful argument for regulation comes from a surprising source. Dietrich Stephan, cofounder and chief science officer of Navigenics, says that his company has had discussions with the Food and Drug Administration and determined that "right now we are exempt from FDA regulation." But he says his company would welcome FDA oversight because there are "a lot of charlatans and pseudoscience occupying this space and we are ready to be regulated."

Competing interests: none declared.

[References]

1. Herper M, Langreth R. Will you get cancer? *Forbes.com* 2007 Jun 18. www.forbes.com/free_forbes/2007/0618/052.html.
2. Bach PB, Jett JR, Pastorino U, Tockman MS, Swensen SJ, Begg CB. Computed tomography screening and lung cancer outcomes. *JAMA* 2007;297:953-61.
3. Barrette S, Bernstein ML, Leclerc JM, Champagne MA, Samson Y, Brossard J, et al. Treatment complications in children diagnosed with neuroblastoma during a screening program. *J Clin Oncol* 2006;24:1542-5.
4. Woods WG, Gao RN, Shuster JJ, Robison LL, Bernstein M, Weitzman S, et al. Screening of infants and mortality due to neuroblastoma. *N Engl J Med* 2002;346:1041-6.
5. Goldstein NM, Kollef MH, Ward S, Gage BF. The impact of the introduction of a rapid D-dimer assay on the diagnostic evaluation of suspected pulmonary embolism. *Arch Intern Med* 2001;161:567-71.
6. Feero WG, Guttmacher AE, Collins FS. The genome gets personal—almost. *JAMA* 2008;299:1351-2.
7. Berg AO, et al. Recommendations from the EGAPP Working Group: testing for cytochrome P450 polymorphisms in adults with nonpsychotic depression treated with selective serotonin reuptake inhibitors. *Gen Med* 2007;91:819-25.

8. Scheuner MT, Sieverding P, Shekelle PG. Delivery of genomic medicine for common chronic adult diseases: a systematic review. *JAMA* 2008;299:1320-34.

9. Welch HG, Burke W. Uncertainties in genetic testing for chronic disease. *JAMA* 1998;280:1525-7.

10. National Cancer Institute. United States cancer statistics: 2004 incidence and mortality. *Surveillance Epidemiology and End Results Database.* http://seer.cancer.gov/faststats.

11. Lu E, Lurie P. Comment on the draft report on the US system of oversight of genetic testing (HRG publication #1832). *Public Citizen* 2007 Dec 21. www.citizen.org/publications/release.cfm?ID=7557.

12. Hudson K, Lurie P, Terry S. Petition requesting a genetic testing specialty and standards for proficiency testing (HRG publication #1787). *Public Citizen* 2006 Sep 26. www.citizen.org/publications/release.cfm?ID=7463.

13. Human Genetics Commission. *More genes direct.* London: Human Genetics Commission, 2007. www.hgc.gov.uk/UploadDocs/DocPub/Document/More%20Genes%20Direct%20-%20final.pdf.

VIEWPOINT 4

"The only thing worse than the paternalism keeping genetic data and its implications from consumers is the failure of imagination this represents, in terms of the potential upside of the coming genomic revolution."

Consumer Genetic Testing Does Not Need Additional Regulation

Christopher Mims

In the following viewpoint, Christopher Mims argues that the US Food and Drug Administration's move toward regulation of the direct-to-consumer genetic testing industry constitutes misguided and unnecessary paternalism. Mims claims that there is no good reason to shield individuals from knowledge of their own genome, and he claims that people will get the information regardless of US regulation of the industry. Mims is a contributing editor at Technology Review, *a columnist at BBC Future, and the editor of the* Smart News *blog at Smithsonian.com.*

Christopher Mims, "Tell Me What's in My Genome!," *Slate*, November 25, 2011.

As you read, consider the following questions:

1. According to the author, what did the Food and Drug Administration tell genetic testing companies in letters sent in June 2010?
2. As an example of the endorsement of genetic exceptionalism, the author cites what 1997 treaty?
3. Addressing the concern about interpretation of genetic information, Mims said the worst-case scenario is what?

Right now, for about the same price as a conventional medical test that reveals just a handful of genes, you could learn the entire contents of your genome. Sure, it's a "research" scan, which means it will contain mistakes, and your insurance won't cover the $4,000–$5,000 bill. But it won't be more than a few years before a complete and virtually error-free version of your genome will be within financial reach. Wouldn't you like to unlock your complete instruction set, with all the medical and ancestry data it contains?

Regulatory Barriers to Genetic Testing

Enticing as that may be, it won't be easy to get those keys if the FDA [Food and Drug Administration] has its way. Last summer [2011], the agency indicated that it wants to classify the work of any company that helps you decipher your genome as a medical test that must be regulated accordingly. But over the last year, the agency's lack of continued communication has left companies that would interpret genetic information—which are simply offering information—confused as to where they stand. This lack of clarity and direction could ultimately mean ceding leadership in this field to overseas competitors who are not similarly constrained.

The FDA has indicated through its public statements that it will put regulatory barriers in the path of companies that want to help us interpret genomes. In June 2010 the agency sent a series of letters to providers like 23andMe, warning them that they were selling what amounted to medical tests that were not vetted by the FDA, and so were in violation of the law. The FDA's letter to consumer genetics testing company 23andMe is a good example of the tack the agency is now taking. "23andMe has never submitted information on the analytical or clinical validity of its tests to FDA for clearance or approval. . . . Consumers may make medical decisions in reliance on this [genetic] information [provided by 23andMe]."

Since then, the FDA has continued to send out letters of a similar tone—23 in total, all to different companies—but has offered no other guidance to providers of direct-to-consumer genetic tests, leaving these companies, and their investors, in the dark about the ultimate direction of regulation in this area. Frustrated by the delay, in recent months many of these companies have made their responses to the FDA public on their websites, in part to protest the climate of ongoing regulatory uncertainty that the agency's actions have created. Others have preemptively eliminated medically significant interpretations from their tests, even if the genes they return still contain that information.

Rather than protect consumers, the FDA's move has left the genetic information industry in limbo—and it seems a matter of time before it moves overseas. Can't get your full genome scan interpreted by software hosted on servers in the United States, owned by a U.S. company? Within a decade, a company in a country not subject to our laws will almost certainly be happy to accommodate you. That's if you don't take the do-it-yourself route first, plumbing your genome with free and open-source software linked to Wikipedia-style databases maintained by volunteers (which, because they aren't sold, aren't subject to FDA regulation).

The Time to Regulate

The FDA [Food and Drug Administration] is being misled by some bioethicists who continue to believe that they can foresee how people will react to new technologies (always negatively) and professional organizations who want to stamp out their competition. If it turns out that down the road some genetic test results in some kind of real harm, that will be the time to start regulating it.

Ronald Bailey,
"Regulating Personal Genomics to Death,"
Reason.com, October 12, 2010.

The Concern About Genetic Information

It's difficult, if not impossible, to find legal or medical scholars in the United States who are against patient access to full genome sequences. So where does the FDA's reticence come from? In part, it's the long shadow of "genetic exceptionalism"—the idea that "genetic information is inherently unique and should be treated differently in law than other forms of personal or medical information," as Alan Dow, vice president and legal counsel at Complete Genomics, put it.

Other Western governments, too, have fallen into the genetic exceptionalism trap. In 1997, the European Union's member states even signed a treaty, the Convention on Human Rights and Biomedicine, which mandates that all signatories apply the precautionary principle when handling biomedical advances like genetic sequencing. This means it's incumbent upon the advocates of these technologies to prove they won't do any harm. So, for example, Germany has instituted a law so broad that it basically prevents anyone from getting her own genes sequenced without a doctor's permission. If the genome-interpreting industry is forced by regulatory limbo to seek shelter outside the United States, we may see developing countries like India compete to fill the market gap.

Based on how we've (mis)used other medical technologies, it's understandable that governmental bodies are at least a little concerned about the advent of whole-genome sequencing. For example, full-body MRI scans have fed into hypochondria-type fears by flagging benign abnormalities that then have to be further examined. Wouldn't a full-genome scan, with the many disease-contributing genes it turns up, do the same? And won't patients who discover, for example, an elevated chance of an incurable disease have their quality of life adversely affected? We'll get to the details later, but the short answer is no.

Paternalism Based on Unfounded Fears

Genetic data have to be interpreted in a way that the public might not be accustomed to. But it is elitism of the highest order to imagine that most of us are simpletons who can't grasp the concept that a gene might contribute to a disease condition, but in no way guarantees it. The fear is that every new study associating a gene with a particular disorder will send patients running to their doctors to ask whether they should be worried. But that seems to be a short-term concern: Most patients will understand the reality after their first (or maybe second) panicked trip to the doctor. The physician will tell them that these studies are always preliminary and that even if they're borne out by subsequent research, the vast majority of these genes have only a marginal effect on our health.

Studies suggest that even patients who find out they have an elevated risk for a disease with a strong genetic component but no cure—like Alzheimer's—handle the news quite well. In light of this, it seems like the worst-case scenario for a full-genome scan is that a patient might be inspired to actually talk to their doctor about their health. If having genes that suggest an elevated chance of heart disease inspire someone to at least be conscientious about their other risk factors for the disease, great! Preliminary research suggests that results of genetic tests change consumers' intention to do something about their health, if not their actual behavior. (Consumers' options about what to do with this information often come down to common lifestyle changes like diet and exercise, which are difficult to get patients to implement under any circumstances.)

The only thing worse than the paternalism keeping genetic data and its implications from consumers is the failure of imagination this represents, in terms of the potential upside of the coming genomic revolution. The more full-genome scans we have, and the cheaper they become, the more useful information patients will have. Widespread genotyping will help us understand our own ancestry, but perhaps more importantly will lead to a new kind of engagement with our health and biology. For this new technology to transform American health—and to cultivate a new, high-tech, high-promise industry within the United States—the FDA needs to provide clarity and guidance. The alternative is that the FDA becomes something like the recording industry at the dawn of the MP3 age: a body trying to lock down immaterial assets that consumers are going to get their hands on, one way or another.

Viewpoint 5

"The only real solution to prevent global food governance and our bodies from having to consume genetically altered foods is to mandate the proper labeling of all foods and to buy local and organic foods."

The US, the UN and Genetic Engineering

Chuck Norris

In the following viewpoint, Chuck Norris argues that all genetically altered foods should be labeled as such. Norris contends that neither the US government nor any international body should enact guidelines that would prohibit consumers from knowledge about genetically engineered products or ingredients, which he claims are unsafe for consumption and the production of which threaten to contaminate organic crops. Norris is a columnist for the online news site WND, a martial artist, and an actor.

As you read, consider the following questions:

1. According to Norris, what percentage of American processed food contains genetically modified ingredients?

2. Norris claims that the US Department of Agriculture wants to eliminate any controls from the genetic alteration of what two crops?
3. Norris implies that the labeling of genetically altered foods will have what impact on the supply and demand of these foods?

Would you know if you were eating genetically engineered foods?

The *Chicago Tribune* recently reported that with no labeling on such foods, many people don't realize that they are doing just that. Genetically modified crops constitute 93 percent of soy, 86 percent of corn and 93 percent of canola seeds planted in the U.S. and are used in about 70 percent of American processed food.

The *Tribune* went on to say that polls from the Pew Center, Consumers Union and Harris Interactive over the past decade have shown that the overwhelming majority of Americans would like to see genetically modified foods better regulated and labeled. Despite that, President Barack Obama's administration has approved an "unprecedented number of genetically modified crops," such as corn grown for ethanol.

The U.S. government is not the only entity boosting and green-lighting genetic engineering of our crops and foods. In 1963, the Food and Agriculture Organization of the United Nations and the World Health Organization adopted the Codex Alimentarius, the food code created by the Codex Alimentarius Commission, whose self-proclaimed mission was to protect health, remove trade obstacles and establish food guidelines. The commission now has 185 members, including the U.S.

Hundreds of guidelines have been adopted by the CAC, in areas ranging from additives to pesticides to, most recently, vitamin and mineral supplements. And this year, it is tackling the issue of whether to label genetically altered and engineered fruits and vegetables.

According to the Alliance for Natural Health, the natural health community has expressed concern about the CAC's guidelines regarding supplements because of parts of the Codex's preamble that "essentially discount the benefits from dietary supplements, and the fact that the scope of the Codex guidelines includes developing minimum and maximum levels of vitamins and minerals."

Though regulating those maximum levels is prohibited by U.S. policy—because dietary supplements are not categorized as drugs—it is one more sign that global governance of our foods is right around the corner. As if American households relinquishing their health and fitness habits to Washington weren't enough, now the entire U.S. needs to be governed by a global food and drug administration?

U.S. food policy may not acquiesce to worldwide regulations tomorrow, but global control is a slippery slope that often is brought about through small steps, or so-called benign increments. The European Union already has enacted many universal food tenets into law. Could the U.S. be that far behind in this global age? In an era in which caving to international pressure is in vogue, how far behind are our food factories?

But does the U.S. really want foreign entities telling us how to eat, what vitamins to take, and how (not) to label U.S. food, now or in the distant future? I'll say what I said in a previous article: The sooner we quit relinquishing our health and fitness responsibilities to the government and take control of our own lives the better off we'll be.

Americans have a right to be concerned with international influence over labeling, marketing and masking the truths behind foods coming from abroad. Our health and welfare should not be turned over to foreign powers, lobbying groups,

Americans Support Labeling of Genetically Modified Foods

Should the federal government require labeling for any foods with genetically modified ingredients?

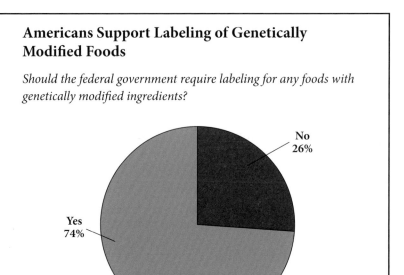

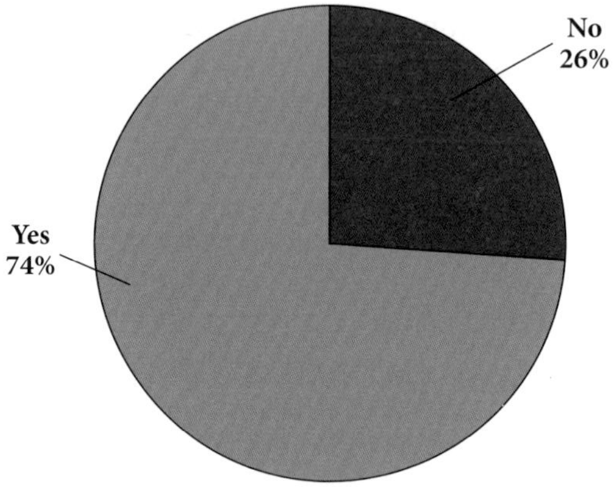

TAKEN FROM: Rasmussen Reports, May 27–28, 2012.

the Food and Drug Administration or the U.S. Department of Agriculture. If that were to happen, we could kiss goodbye the freedoms we've long enjoyed with dietary supplements and organic foods.

The added difficulty with genetic tampering and labels is that we know big business and lobbying often control the decisions in Washington. Recently, that was made evident again by the actions of the USDA. Despite the fact that tests prove that genetically engineered organisms become a part of the bacteria in our digestive tracts, the Alliance for Natural Health reported how the USDA now wants to eliminate any controls from genetically altered corn and cotton.

The ANH cited the wisdom of the late George Wald, a Nobel laureate in physiology or medicine and one of the first scientists to speak out about the dangers of genetically engineered foods:

> "Recombinant DNA technology (genetic engineering) faces our society with problems unprecedented, not only in the history of science, but of life on the Earth. . . . Now whole new proteins will be transposed overnight into wholly new associations, with consequences no one can foretell, either for the host organism or their neighbors. . . . For going ahead in this direction may not only be unwise but dangerous. Potentially, it could breed new animal and plant diseases, new sources of cancer, novel epidemics."

Fourteen states have introduced legislation on genetically modified organism labeling, but most face governmental gridlock. So please, take action and keep foods safe (non–genetically engineered) by contacting your representatives, as well as the FDA and the USDA, and demanding that genetically modified food be labeled as such. In addition, corn and cotton must not be deregulated. Without strict controls, as the ANH concludes, genetically engineered crops will encroach on non–genetically engineered crops, contaminating them and rendering the organic crops non-organic.

The only real solution to prevent global food governance and our bodies from having to consume genetically altered foods is to mandate the proper labeling of all foods and to buy local and organic foods. By diminishing the supply of and demand for imported and genetically engineered foods, we can diminish their tyranny at the borders of our bodies.

VIEWPOINT 6

> *"Product labeling that conveys essential information is important, but mandatory labeling of gene-spliced foods is a bad idea."*

Labeling of Genetically Modified Foods Is Unnecessary and Unconstitutional

Henry I. Miller and Gregory Conko

In the following viewpoint, Henry I. Miller and Gregory Conko argue that government-mandated labeling of genetically modified foods would convey irrelevant information and would be a violation of the First Amendment. Miller and Conko claim that gene-spliced foods are safe and not very different from most other crops that have been genetically modified in some manner. Miller is a physician and molecular biologist, as well as a fellow at Stanford University's Hoover Institution. Conko is a senior fellow at the Competitive Enterprise Institute. Miller and Conko are coauthors of The Frankenfood Myth: How Protest and Politics Threaten the Biotech Revolution.

Henry I. Miller and Gregory Conko, "Labeling of Biotech Foods Is Unnecessary and Unconstitutional," *Forbes*, December 8, 2011.

As you read, consider the following questions:

1. Miller and Conko contend that the demand for government-mandated labeling of genetically modified foods unfairly targets what particular technique?
2. The authors contend that more than how many acres of gene-spliced crops have been cultivated worldwide?
3. According to the authors, on what basis did a federal court determine that dairy products did not need to be labeled as containing a gene-spliced protein?

Should the government require that labels on cans of marinara sauce contain information about whether the tomatoes in it were hand- or machine-picked? No way! Ridiculous and irrelevant, you'd say. Right on all counts. But that label makes as little sense as the demands of food activist and *Forbes* contributor Michelle Maisto.

The Call for Mandatory Labeling

Maisto's latest *Forbes* article [December 1, 2011] calls for compulsory, government-mandated labels to indicate foods that have been genetically improved. Yet the foods that Maisto wants to target are those manipulated with the most modern and precise gene-splicing techniques—and only those techniques. Such labels would not only put groundless fears ahead of science—promoting ignorance and hysteria among consumers—they would also be unconstitutional.

Product labeling that conveys essential information is important, but mandatory labeling of gene-spliced foods is a bad idea. First, it implies risks for which there is no evidence. Second, it flies in the face of worldwide scientific consensus about the appropriate basis of regulation, which focuses palpable risks, not the use of certain techniques. Third, it would push the costs of product development into the stratosphere. Finally, the requirement would constitute a punitive tax on a superior technology.

Maisto is misinformed in so many ways.

The Safety of Gene-Spliced Foods

Let's begin with her assertion that there's "a lot of debate about whether or not it's safe to eat GM [genetically modified] foods." In the parlance of Maisto and other radical food activists, "GM" refers to products that come from plants, animals or microorganisms crafted with sophisticated gene-splicing techniques, in which genes are moved around precisely and predictably. Without any scientific basis, the term implies that gene splicing is a meaningful "category" and that its use somehow gives rise to products the risks of which are higher or more uncertain than other techniques for genetic modification. However, a broad and decades-long scientific consensus holds that modern techniques of genetic modification are an extension, or refinement—that is, an improvement—on the kinds of genetic modification that have long been used to enhance plants, microorganisms, and animals for food.

One has to wonder whether Maisto knows that with the exception of wild game, wild berries, wild mushrooms and fish and shellfish, all the plant- and animal-derived foods in our diets—even the overpriced organic stuff at Whole Foods—have resulted from genetic modification that employs techniques that are far less precise and predictable than the ones that concern her. Likewise, is she aware that every major scientific and public health organization that has studied gene splicing—from the American Medical Association to the National Academy of Sciences and dozens more—has concluded that gene-spliced foods are at least as safe, and probably safer, than conventional ones?

The safety record of gene-spliced plants and foods derived from them is extraordinary. After the cultivation of more than 3 billion acres (cumulatively) of gene-spliced crops worldwide and the consumption of more than 3 *trillion* servings of food and food ingredients from such crops by inhabitants of North America alone, there has not been a single ecosystem disrupted or a single confirmed adverse reaction.

What are the advantages of gene-spliced crops? Every year, farmers planting gene-spliced varieties spray millions fewer gallons of chemical pesticides and prevent less erosion of topsoil. In addition, many gene-spliced varieties are less susceptible to mold infection and have lower levels of fungal toxins, making them safer for consumers and livestock.

No Requirement for Irrelevant Information

Now let's get to the labeling issue.

Maisto complains that "food can be tinkered with at the DNA level and no one is obligated to say so." True, but irrelevant. For one thing, with the exceptions mentioned above, all the foods in our diet have been altered "at the DNA level"—because that's how changes in organisms occur. When plant breeders cross a tangerine with a grapefruit to get a tangelo or construct a variety of potato resistant to viruses, the genetic changes are mediated by alterations in the DNA.

There are good reasons that such "tinkering at the DNA level" need not be revealed on labels. Federal regulation requires that food labels be truthful and not misleading and prohibits label statements that could be misunderstood, even if they are strictly accurate. For example, although a "cholesterol-free" label on a certain variety or batch of fresh spinach would be accurate, it transgresses the FDA's [Food and Drug Administration's] rules because it could be interpreted as implying that spinach usually contains cholesterol, which it does not.

Following long-standing precedents in food regulation, the FDA requires labeling only to indicate that a new food raises questions of safety, nutrition or proper usage. But instead of educating or serving a legitimate consumers' "need to know" certain information, mandatory labels on gene-spliced food would imply a warning.

An Unconstitutional Requirement

The FDA's approach to labeling has been upheld both directly and indirectly by various federal court decisions that have consistently struck down mandatory labeling not supported by data. In the early 1990s, a group of Wisconsin consumers sued the FDA, arguing that the agency's decision not to require the labeling of dairy products from cows treated with a gene-spliced protein called bovine somatotropin, or bST, allowed those products to be labeled in a false and misleading manner. (In other words, the plaintiffs wanted the same sort of mandatory labeling advocated by Maisto.) However, because the plaintiffs failed to demonstrate any material difference between milk from treated and untreated cows, the federal court agreed with the FDA, finding that "it would be misbranding to label the product as different, even if consumers misperceived the product as different."

In another federal case, several food associations and companies challenged a Vermont statute that required labeling to identify milk from cows treated with gene-spliced bST. The U.S. Second Circuit Court of Appeals ruled that a labeling mandate grounded in consumer perception rather than in a product's measurable characteristics raises serious constitutional concerns. Namely, it violates commercial free speech. The court found both the labeling statute and companion regulations unconstitutional because they forced producers to make involuntary statements when there was no material reason to do so.

What's more, consumers don't need a mandatory "GM" label: The First Amendment protects the right of food purveyors to sell *non*-gene-spliced products and to advertise that fact to consumers by means of labeling. (This would be similar to the way that halal and kosher products are offered to consumers.)

Periodical and Internet Sources Bibliography

The following articles have been selected to supplement the diverse views presented in this chapter.

Ronald Bailey	"I'll Show You My Genome. Will You Show Me Yours?," *Reason*, January 2011.
William Y. Brown	"It's Time for a New Biotechnology Law," Brookings Institution, July 27, 2011.
Shannon Brownlee	"Google's Guinea Pigs," *Mother Jones*, November/December 2009.
Marcy Darnovsky	"Voluntary Isn't Working: Recent Events Show Need for Regulation of Assisted Reproduction," *Modern Healthcare*, April 13, 2009.
Henry Greely	"The Genetics of Fear," *Democracy: A Journal of Ideas*, Summer 2008.
Michael Hansen	"Labeling of Food Made for AquAdvantage Salmon," ConsumersUnion.org, September 21, 2010.
Gregory Jaffe	"Regulatory Procedure Necessary for GE Food," *Hill*, October 1, 2010.
Sara Katsanis and Gail Javitt	"Surreptitious DNA Testing," Genetics & Public Policy Center, January 2009.
Henry I. Miller	"Back to the Future: Let's Reverse 25 Years of Flawed Agbiotech Regulation," *Forbes*, June 22, 2011.
Sam Ross-Brown	"GM Food: Don't Ask, Don't Tell?," *Utne Reader*, May 8, 2012.
Washington Post	"Labels May Not Be Necessary on Genetically Altered Foods," September 23, 2010.

For Further Discussion

Chapter 1

1. Jeffrey Scott Coker and John Nichols have conflicting views on genetic engineering. Coker views the process as natural, whereas Nichols sees it as a threat to agriculture. Which author do you think makes the stronger argument? Defend your answer with support from the text.
2. In 2009 President Barack Obama lifted the ban on federal funding for stem cell research. Ken Blackwell argues that this will open the door to human cloning. Do you agree with Blackwell? Explain your reasoning.

Chapter 2

1. The Institute for Responsible Technology raises concerns about the health effects of genetically modified (GM) food, whereas Henry I. Miller raises concerns about the health effects of *not* using genetic engineering in crops. Who has the stronger argument? Defend your answer with textual support.
2. Jesse Reynolds argues that greater regulation is needed for the fertility industry, whereas Greg Beato says that freedom from government interference leads to innovation. One main principle at work in justifying regulation of the industry is the prevention of harm. Does this principle support greater regulation for the fertility industry, based on what Reynolds and Beato argue? Explain.

Chapter 3

1. Mark Tapson clearly expresses distaste for the proposal of S. Matthew Liao to genetically engineer humans to be smaller, but does Tapson have a good argument in opposition? Why or why not?

2. Anne Minard argues that genetically engineered pigs could provide environmental benefits, whereas Lucy Sharratt maintains that such pigs are not a good solution for environmental problems. Which author do you think makes the stronger argument? Cite examples from the text to support your reasoning.

Chapter 4

1. Richard Hayes argues that regulation of genetic engineering is necessary, whereas Ronald Bailey argues against new regulation. Utilizing the reasoning of one of these authors, explain why genetic modification of humans for skin color either should or should not be regulated.
2. In support of his view that regulation of genetic testing is unnecessary, Christopher Mims argues that consumers will get their genetic information somewhere else. Create an analogous argument for why drugs should be legal. Is this reasoning effective in each case? Why or why not?

Organizations to Contact

The editors have compiled the following list of organizations concerned with the issues debated in this book. The descriptions are derived from materials provided by the organizations. All have publications or information available for interested readers. The list was compiled on the date of publication of the present volume; the information provided here may change. Be aware that many organizations take several weeks or longer to respond to inquiries, so allow as much time as possible.

American Society of Human Genetics (ASHG)
9650 Rockville Pike, Bethesda, MD 20814-3998
(301) 634-7300 • fax: (301) 634-7079
e-mail: society@ashg.org
website: www.ashg.org

The American Society of Human Genetics (ASHG) is the primary professional membership organization for human genetics specialists worldwide. ASHG provides forums for advancing genetic research, enhancing genetics education, and promoting responsible scientific policies. ASHG publishes the *American Journal of Human Genetics* and the electronic newsletter *SNP-IT*.

American Society of Law, Medicine & Ethics (ASLME)
765 Commonwealth Avenue, Suite 1634, Boston, MA 02215
(617) 262-4990 • fax: (617) 437-7596
e-mail: info@aslme.org
website: www.aslme.org

The American Society of Law, Medicine & Ethics (ASLME) is a nonprofit educational organization focused on the intersection of law, medicine, and ethics. ASLME aims to provide a forum to exchange ideas in order to protect public health, reduce health disparities, promote quality of care, and facilitate dialogue on emerging science. ASLME publishes two journals: *Journal of Law, Medicine & Ethics* and *American Journal of Law & Medicine*.

Biotechnology Industry Organization (BIO)
1201 Maryland Avenue SW, Suite 900, Washington, DC 20024
(202) 962-9200 • fax: (202) 488-6301
e-mail: info@bio.org
website: www.bio.org

The Biotechnology Industry Organization (BIO) represents biotechnology companies, academic institutions, state biotechnology centers, and related organizations that support the use of biotechnology. BIO advocates for its corporate members by championing the use of biotechnology. BIO publishes advocacy on issues related to genetic engineering, including "Feeding the World: How to Feed Seven Billion People."

Center for Bioethics & Human Dignity (CBHD)
Trinity International University, 2065 Half Day Road
Deerfield, IL 60015
(847) 317-8180 • fax: (847) 317-8101
e-mail: info@cbhd.org
website: www.cbhd.org

The Center for Bioethics & Human Dignity (CBHD) works to bring explicit Christian engagement into the bioethics arena. CBHD seeks to equip thought leaders to engage the issues of bioethics using the tools of rigorous research, conceptual analysis, charitable critique, leading-edge publications, and effective teaching. Among CBHD's information available at its website are reports and podcasts, including the podcast "Human Dignity and Biomedicine."

Center for Food Safety (CFS)
660 Pennsylvania Avenue SE, Suite 302
Washington, DC 20003
(202) 547-9359 • fax: (202) 547-9429
e-mail: office@centerforfoodsafety.org
website: www.centerforfoodsafety.org

The Center for Food Safety (CFS) is a nonprofit public interest organization established for the purpose of challenging harmful food production technologies and promoting sustainable alternatives. CFS combines multiple tools and strategies in pursuing its goals, including litigation and legal petitions for rule making and legal support for various sustainable agriculture and food safety constituencies, as well as public education, grassroots organizing, and media outreach. CFS publishes reports and fact sheets, available at its website, including "'Agent Orange' Corn: The Next Stage in the Chemical Arms Race."

Center for Genetics and Society (CGS)
1936 University Avenue, Suite 350, Berkeley, CA 94704
(510) 665-7760 • fax: (510) 665-8760
e-mail: info@geneticsandsociety.org
website: www.geneticsandsociety.org

The Center for Genetics and Society (CGS) is a nonprofit information and public affairs organization working to encourage responsible uses and effective societal governance of human genetic and reproductive technologies. CGS works with scientists, health professionals, and civil society leaders to oppose applications of new human genetic and reproductive technologies that objectify and commodify human life and threaten to divide human society. CGS publishes reports, articles, and newsletters, including the report "Playing the Gene Card? A Report on Race and Human Biotechnology."

Council for Responsible Genetics (CRG)
5 Upland Road, Suite 3, Cambridge, MA 02140
(617) 868-0870 • fax: (617) 491-5344
e-mail: crg@gene-watch.org
website: www.councilforresponsiblegenetics.org

The Council for Responsible Genetics (CRG) is a nonprofit organization dedicated to fostering public debate about the social, ethical, and environmental implications of genetic technologies. CRG works through the media and concerned citizens to distribute accurate information and represent the public interest on emerging issues in biotechnology. CRG publishes *GeneWatch*, a magazine dedicated to monitoring biotechnology's social, ethical, and environmental consequences.

Ethics and Public Policy Center (EPPC)
1730 M Street NW, Suite 910, Washington, DC 20036
(202) 682-1200 • fax: (202) 408-0632
e-mail: ethics@eppc.org
website: www.eppc.org

The Ethics and Public Policy Center (EPPC) is dedicated to applying the Judeo-Christian moral tradition to critical issues of public policy. Through its core programs, such as Bioethics and American Democracy, EPPC and its scholars work to influence policy makers and to transform the culture through the world of ideas. EPPC publishes the *New Atlantis*, a quarterly journal about technology with an emphasis on bioethics.

Food & Water Watch
1616 P Street NW, Suite 300, Washington, DC 20036
(202) 683-2500 • fax: (202) 683-2501
e-mail: info@fwwatch.org
website: www.foodandwaterwatch.org

Food & Water Watch works to ensure the food and water supply is safe, accessible, and sustainably produced. Food & Water Watch promotes policies that lead to sustainable, healthy food; advocates for safe and affordable drinking water; and promotes policies that maintain the environmental quality of the ocean. Food & Water Watch publishes fact sheets and reports such as "The Case for GE Labeling."

Genetics and Public Policy Center
Johns Hopkins University, Berman Institute of Bioethics
1717 Massachusetts Avenue NW, Suite 530
Washington, DC 20036
(202) 663-5971 • fax: (202) 663-5992
e-mail: gppcnews@jhu.edu
website: www.dnapolicy.org

The Genetics and Public Policy Center works to help policy makers, the press, and the public understand the challenges and opportunities of genetic medicine. The center conducts legal research and policy analysis, performs policy-relevant social science research, crafts policy recommendations, and influences national genetics policy. Available at the center's website are numerous reports and testimony transcripts, including the report "The Genetic Town Hall: Public Opinion About Research on Genes, Environment, and Health."

Institute for Responsible Technology

PO Box 469, Fairfield, IA 52556
(641) 209-1765
e-mail: info@responsibletechnology.org
website: www.responsibletechnology.org

The Institute for Responsible Technology is an organization that works to educate policy makers and the public about genetically modified organisms (GMOs). The institute investigates and reports on the risks of GMOs and their impact on health, the environment, the economy, and agriculture, as well as the problems associated with current research, regulation, corporate practices, and reporting. The institute has several resources available at its website, including brochures, reports, videos, and an archive of its *Spilling the Beans* newsletter.

National Human Genome Research Institute (NHGRI)

National Institutes of Health, Building 31, Room 4B09
31 Center Drive, MSC 2152, Bethesda, MD 20892-2152
(301) 402-0911 • fax: (301) 402-2218
website: www.genome.gov

The National Human Genome Research Institute (NHGRI) led the National Institutes of Health's contribution to the international Human Genome Project, which had as its primary goal the sequencing of the human genome. NHGRI supports the development of resources and technology that will accelerate genome research and its application to human health. NHGRI has many educational tools available at its website, including the multimedia "Understanding the Human Genome Project."

Union of Concerned Scientists (UCS)
2 Brattle Square, Cambridge, MA 02138-3780
(617) 547-5552 • fax: (617) 864-9405
website: www.ucsusa.org

The Union of Concerned Scientists (UCS) is a science-based nonprofit organization working for a healthy environment and a safer world. UCS combines independent scientific research and citizen action to develop innovative, practical solutions and to secure responsible changes in government policy, corporate practices, and consumer choices. UCS publishes numerous reports, including "High and Dry: Why Genetic Engineering Is Not Solving Agriculture's Drought Problem in a Thirsty World."

US Food and Drug Administration (FDA)
10903 New Hampshire Avenue, Silver Spring, MD 20993
(888) 463-6332
website: www.fda.gov

The Food and Drug Administration (FDA) is an agency within the US Department of Health and Human Services. The FDA is responsible for protecting public health by assuring food and drug safety. The FDA's website contains a variety of information on its regulations as well as food and drug safety.

Bibliography of Books

Carol Isaacson Barash	*Just Genes: The Ethics of Genetic Technologies*. Westport, CT: Praeger, 2008.
Roberta M. Berry	*The Ethics of Genetic Engineering*. New York: Routledge, 2007.
Claire Hope Cummings	*Uncertain Peril: Genetic Engineering and the Future of Seeds*. Boston, MA: Beacon Press, 2008.
Neal D. Fortin	*Food Regulation: Law, Science, Policy, and Practice*. Hoboken, NJ: John Wiley & Sons, 2009.
Masha Gessen	*Blood Matters: From Inherited Illness to Designer Babies, How the World and I Found Ourselves in the Future of the Gene*. Orlando, FL: Harcourt, 2008.
Jonathan Glover	*Choosing Children: Genes, Disability, and Design*. New York: Oxford University Press, 2006.
John Harris	*Enhancing Evolution: The Ethical Case for Making Better People*. Princeton, NJ: Princeton University Press, 2007.
Matti Häyry	*Rationality and the Genetic Challenge: Making People Better?* New York: Cambridge University Press, 2010.

Craig Holdrege and Steve Talbott — *Beyond Biotechnology: The Barren Promise of Genetic Engineering*. Lexington: University Press of Kentucky, 2010.

Lori P. Knowles and Gregory E. Kaebnick, eds. — *Reprogenetics: Law, Policy, and Ethical Issues*. Baltimore, MD: Johns Hopkins University Press, 2007.

B. Andrew Lustig, Baruch A. Brody, and Gerald P. McKenny, eds. — *Altering Nature*. New York: Springer, 2008.

H. Daniel Monsour, ed. — *Ethics and the New Genetics: An Integrated Approach*. Toronto: University of Toronto Press, 2007.

Pete Moore — *Enhancing Me: The Hope and the Hype of Human Enhancement*. Hoboken, NJ: Wiley, 2008.

Thomas H. Murray, Karen J. Maschke, Angela A. Wasunna, eds. — *Performance-Enhancing Technologies in Sports: Ethical, Conceptual, and Scientific Issues*. Baltimore, MD: Johns Hopkins University Press, 2009.

Marion Nestle — *Safe Food: The Politics of Food Safety*. Berkeley: University of California Press, 2010.

Robert Paarlberg — *Food Politics: What Everyone Needs to Know*. New York: Oxford University Press, 2010.

Marie-Monique Robin	*The World According to Monsanto: Pollution, Corruption, and the Control of the World's Food Supply*. New York: New Press, 2010.
Pamela C. Ronald and Raoul W. Adamchak	*Tomorrow's Table: Organic Farming, Genetics, and the Future of Food*. New York: Oxford University Press, 2008.
Michael J. Sandel	*The Case Against Perfection: Ethics in the Age of Genetic Engineering*. Cambridge, MA: Belknap Press, 2007.
Julian Savulescu and Nick Bostrom, eds.	*Human Enhancement*. New York: Oxford University Press, 2009.
Frida Simonstein	*Reprogen-Ethics and the Future of Gender*. New York: Springer, 2009.
Jeffrey M. Smith	*Genetic Roulette: The Documented Health Risks of Genetically Engineered Foods*. Fairfield, IA: Yes! Books, 2007.
Terry L. Smith	*Modern Genetic Science: New Technology, New Decisions*. New York: Rosen, 2009.
Michael Specter	*Denialism: How Irrational Thinking Hinders Scientific Progress, Harms the Planet, and Threatens Our Lives*. New York: Penguin Press, 2009.
Spencer S. Stober and Donna Yarri	*God, Science, and Designer Genes: An Exploration of Emerging Genetic Technologies*. Santa Barbara, CA: Praeger, 2009.

Linda Tagliaferro *Genetic Engineering: Modern Progress or Future Peril?* Minneapolis, MN: Twenty-First Century Books, 2010.

Index

A

Abortion politics, 160
Abortion rights, 106, 161, 168
Abraham Centre of Life, 54
Adamchak, Raoul, 87
African agriculture, 90, 99
Agribusiness and factory farming
- biopharming, 38, 42, 44
- hog farming, 145, 146, 147, 148

Agricultural dilemmas
- breadth of solutions, 26–27
- environmental harm, 86, 99–100
- improved/solved with genetic engineering, 20, 22–25, 85–91

Agriculture
- dangers of crop genetic engineering, 33–45, 74
- diversity diminishment, 24, 26
- economic incentives to farmers, 38, 40, 41–42
- extent of genetic engineering, 15, 23–24, 87, 93, 188
- indigenous systems, 26–27, 98, 99
- non-productivity of genetic modification, 92–100
- political economy, 37–38, 83, 148–149
- proponents of genetic engineering/modification, 20–32, 81–83, 85–91
- *See also* Genetically engineered/modified food; Plants

Agroecological farming, 98
Alberts, Mike, 42
Alfalfa, 74
Algal blooms, 122, 141, 147
Allergic reactions
- decreased, genetically engineered products, 27
- increased, GM foods, 37, 73, 74–75, 76, 78, 98

Alliance for Natural Health, 189, 190–191
Alzheimer's disease, 55, 56, 185
American Academy of Environmental Medicine, 73, 78
American Corn Growers Association, 38
American Farm Bureau Federation, 44
American Medical Association
- bovine somatotropin food products policies, 16
- gene-spliced foods, 194

American Society for Reproductive Medicine (ASRM), 102–103, 106
American Society of Plant Biologists, 22–23
Andersen, Ross, 119–128
Animal cloning
- organ use, 29
- public opinion, 18

Animal feeds
- contamination, 35, 44, 81, 150
- fish, 136
- fumonisin levels, 81, 82–83
- GM foods effects, 75, 82–83

pigs, 142, 143, 146, 148, 149
poultry, 150
Animal insulin, 27
Animal testing, 30, 76–77, 82–83, 143
Animals
avoidance as food, 120, 122–123, 124, 126, 130
genetic engineering for food, 18, 29–30, 134–139, 140–144
human-animal hybrids, 55, 126–127, 166, 169
Annan, Kofi, 160
Antibiotic resistance, 77
Antidiscrimination laws, health, 177
Aquaculture, 134, 136–138
Arms race and control, 160
Arthritis, 15
Assisted reproductive technology
industry profits, 102
regulation is needed, 101–107, 164–166, 167
regulation is not needed, 108–113, 163–169
in vitro fertilization, 47, 50, 54, 104, 109, 123–124, 125, 161*t*, 165
Athletes and genetic engineering, 30–31, 49
Atmospheric emissions. *See* Greenhouse gas emissions
ATryn (anticoagulant), 144
Australia
genetic engineering trials, 25
rBST bans, 154
Avey, Linda, 172–173, 176

B

Bacillus thuringiensis bacteria, crop modification, 24, 74, 76, 77, 89, 93, 116–117
Bacterial DNA, 21
genetically engineered organisms, 143, 146, 190
GM crops and foods, 73, 74, 77, 81–82, 93
Bailey, Ronald, 50, 163–169, 184
Baird, Eisenstadt v. (1972), 168
Bananas, 90
Bans, products and processes
genetically engineered ingredients, 80
human cloning, 66, 166, 167
human enhancement potential, 30, 169
lifted, stem cell research funding, 57, 58, 59, 64–65, 66
rBST (recombinant bovine somatotropin), 16, 154, 155
Barley, 25
Beato, Greg, 108–111
Beauty norms, 105
Beer, 80
Bell, Buck v. (1922), 168
Beyond Bioethics: A Proposal for Modernizing the Regulation of Human Biotechnologies (Fukuyama and Furger), 164, 167
Biofuels production and engineering, 25, 188
Biopharmaceuticals. *See* Pharmaceutical development
Biotechnology Industry Organization, 41
Biowarfare, 160

Birth control laws, 168
Birth defects
causes, 81
treatment, 28
See also Genetic diseases
Blackwell, Ken, 63–67
Borlaug, Norman, 86, 90
Bovine somatotropin (BST)
labeling, 155, 196
use and effects, 15–16, 154–155
BRCA1 gene, 174–175
Breast cancer
genetic screening, 47, 173, 174–175
risks rates, 175
Brin, Sergey, 176
Brownlee, Shannon, 170–179
"Bt" technology and crops, 24, 74, 76, 77, 89, 93–100, 116–117
Buck v. Bell (1922), 168
Burke, Wylie, 174
Bush, George W., 40, 64–65, 66

C

Cady, John, 44
Canada
"Enviropig" and pork, 141–144, 145
hog farms and industry, 148–149, 150–151
rBST bans, 16, 154
regulation standards, 107, 159
Cancer
development, gene therapy, 15, 70–71
genetic screening, 47, 173, 174–175
prevention, human papillomavirus, 27–28
treatment, gene therapy, 28, 70
Canola, 15, 74, 188
Caplan, Art, 103, 105–106
Carbon pricing, 121
Carlsberg (brewer), 80
Catholic Church, beliefs, 52
Center for Genetics and Society, 56, 113, 157
Centers for Disease Control and Prevention (CDC), 102–103
Centers for Medicare and Medicaid Services, 178
Child death, 54
China
genetically engineered cotton, 24, 89
population policy, 125, 131
Church, George, 173, 174
Class inequalities
human genetic engineering would cause, 46, 48–49, 51, 105–106, 112
human genetic engineering would not cause, 108, 112
Climate change
agriculture effects, 26–27, 89, 90, 99–100
crop protections and projections, 85, 87–89
global threat, 55, 90
human causes and responsibilities, 127–128, 129, 130, 133
human genetic engineering is a good solution, 119–128
human genetic engineering is dangerous, 129–133
market solutions, 121–122
Clinical Laboratory Improvement Amendments (1988), 178

Clinical trials, gene therapy, 15, 70–71
Clinton, Bill, 66
Cloning. *See* Animal cloning; Human cloning
Cod, 135
Codex Alimentarius Commission, 188–189
Coker, Jeffrey Scott, 20–32
Collective action problems, 158
Commercial genetic testing
  does not need additional regulation, 181–186
  industry services, and regulation needs, 170–179
Commodification of reproduction
  leading factors and dangers, 49, 50, 55, 161–162
  prevention, 165, 166
Comstock Laws (1873), 168
Confidential business information, 42, 75, 149–150
Conko, Gregory
  genetic engineering activists, criticism, 82
  GM food labeling is unnecessary and unconstitutional, 192–197
Connecticut, Griswold v. (1965), 168
Consumer protections, and needs
  direct-to-consumer genetic screening, 170–179, 183
  GE foods, 18–19, 35, 37, 42–44, 138–139
  See also Food labeling
Contamination dangers
  biopharming, 33–45
  genetically engineered organisms, 150
  natural, 81
  organic farming affected, 37, 187, 191
Contraception laws, 168
Convention on Human Rights and Biomedicine (1997), 184–185
Cooper University Hospital, 176–177
Coriell Institute for Medical Research, 176
Corn
  agricultural productivity, 95–96, 96*t*
  allergies, 76
  animal feeds, 81
  biopharming and contamination, 35–38, 40, 41, 43
  ethanol, 25, 188
  genetically engineered, 15, 23–24, 25, 34–38, 40, 41, 43, 73, 74, 76, 77, 81–82, 82, 93–95, 96*t*, 188, 190, 191
  oversight deregulation, 190, 191
  US industry and economy, 37–38, 95
Corporate control, agriculture
  biotech and dangers, 35, 36–37
  monopolies and dangers, 24, 26
  as relevant but ignored issue, 23
Corporate control, genetic engineering, 53, 55
Corporate control, personal genetic data, 172
Cotton
  allergies, 76
  genetically engineered, 23–24, 25, 74, 76, 89, 190, 191

oversight deregulation, 190, 191
Crop rotation, 98
Cystic fibrosis, 54, 56, 70

D

Daschle, Tom, 44
Data collection, medical records, 175–177
deCODE genetics (company), 171
Deep ecology, 127–128
Deforestation, 122
Demonstrations and protests
criticisms, 80, 82, 83
genetic engineering, 22, 35
"Designer babies"
embryo sales, 54, 165, 166
film portrayals, 48–49
processes, dangers, and criticisms, 49, 50, 101, 102, 104–106, 110, 112, 165
support of processes, 47–48, 51, 104–105, 108–113
Dietary supplements, 189, 190
Disability rights activists, 162
Disease prevention
cancer, 27–28
direct-to-consumer genetic screening, 170–179, 181–186
genetic diseases, 47, 54, 110, 112–113, 167, 168–169
Disease treatment
genetic engineering abilities and benefits, 18, 28–29, 70
risks and failures, 15, 70–71
stem cell research for, 57–62
therapy vs. enhancement, 159
See also Gene therapy; Pharmaceutical development
Dittrich, Keith, 38
DNA, nature of, 21–22
DNA mutation
GM foods, 74
natural processes, 21, 28, 195
Dow, Alan, 184
Dow Chemical, 39–40
Drought-resistant crops, 25, 89
Drug development. *See* Pharmaceutical development
Dyslexia, 48, 51

E

E. coli bacteria, 15–16, 27, 143, 146
Ecological Society of America, 22
Eisenstadt v. Baird (1972), 168
Eli Lilly (company), 41
Embryo destruction, stem cell research, 52, 63–67
Embryo implantation, ethics, 101, 102, 103–104, *104,* 105–106
Embryo screening and selection
Catholic Church stance, 52
designer babies, 48, 101, 102, 104–106, 108–113
disease avoidance, 47, 54, 110, 112–113, 167, 168–169
sales, 54, 165, 166
state laws, 106–107, 113
Embryonic stem cell research. *See* Stem cell research
Embryos, legal designations, 106
Energy efficiency, 120, 123, 126, 130, 131
Enough (McKibben), 49
Environment Canada, 141

Environmental dilemmas
agriculture, and proposed solutions, 22, 86–91, 99–100, 116–117
associated with genetic engineering, 55, 56, 116–118, 119–128, 129–133
genetically engineered foods, 18, 134–139, 140–144
land use and productivity improvements, 25, 26, 90–91, 195
livestock farming and meat consumption, 122–123, 143, 146, 147, 148
technology development, 120
See also Climate change
Environmental Protection Agency, regulations needs, 42, 44
"Enviropig," 140, 141–144, 145, 146–151
Enzymes, 14, 142, 146
Ethics issues
current meat production processes, 30
embryo sales, 54, 165, 166
human clinical trials, 15, 70–71
human genetic engineering, 30–31, 49, 52, 55, 101–107, 164–166, 167, 169
human genetic engineering and the environment, 119, 120–128
stem cell research and embryo destruction, 52, 63–67
Ethics, Policy & Environment (journal), 120, 124, 130
Eugenics
history and present dangers, 48–49, 55, 162
laws, 168
European Commission
Scientific Committee on Animal Health and Animal Welfare, 154–155
Scientific Committee on Veterinary Measures Relating to Public Health, 155
European Union
Convention on Human Rights and Biomedicine (1997), 184–185
genetically modified food import restrictions, 38
rBST bans, 16, 154, 155
regulation strictness, 162, 189
Evolution, 31

F

Factory farming and agribusiness
biopharming, 38, 42, 44
hog farming, 145, 146, 147, 148
Family size, 125–126, 131, 133
FDA. *See* US Food and Drug Administration (FDA)
Fertility medicine. *See* Assisted reproductive technology; In vitro fertilization (IVF)
First Amendment violations, 192, 196–197
Fish, genetically engineered
benefits for people and planet, 134–139
public opinion, 18
Fisheries, 135, 136–138
"Flavr Savr" tomato, 15
Flood-resistant crops, 24, 85, 88–89
Folic acid, 81

Food. *See* Genetically engineered/modified food
Food codes, 188–189
Food insecurity and hunger
genetically engineered organisms, needs, 142
genetically modified crops can end, 85–91
genetically modified crops will not end, 92–100
Food labeling
genetically engineered salmon, 138–139
milk from rBST-treated cows, 155
national policies, 155, 189–190, 195
opposition, 192–197
public opinion, 18–19, 155–156, 188, 190*t*
support, 15, 18–19, 187–191, 190*t*
Food poisoning, 81
Food price increases, 93
Food supplements, 189, 190
For-profit genetic screening, 170–179, 181–186
Forced sterilization, 49, 168
Forsberg, Cecil, 143
Freedom
human genetic engineering and the environment, 119, 125–126, 129, 131–132
human genetic engineering limits, 46, 49, 51, 56
Freese, Bill, 40
Friends of the Earth, 40
Frito-Lay, 80
Fukuyama, Francis, 164–166, 167, 168–169
Fumonisin, 81, 82–83
Fungal toxins in food, 81–83, 195
Furger, Franco, 164, 165, 167

G

Gates, Bill, 87
Gattaca (film), 48–49
GE Food Alert, 37, 40
Gelsinger, Jesse, 15
Gender selection, 110, 165, 166, 168
Gene imprinting, 125
Gene mutation, natural, 21
Gene therapy
failures and deaths, 15, 70–71
genetic engineering benefits, 28–29, 52, 70
genetic engineering oversight, 15, 159
genetic engineering research, 14–15, 70–71
Genentech, 27, 171–172
Genetic diseases
risk calculations, 172, 173
screening, 47, 54, 110, 167, 168–169, 170–179, 181–186
treatment, 28, 29, 173
Genetic engineering
edible organisms, 134–139, 140–144, 145–151
is natural and should be pursued, 20–32
new technology does not need regulation, 108–113, 163–169
new technology needs regulation, 157–162
prevalence, 15, 23–24
processes described, 14, 39
public opinion, 18–19, 20, 22–23, 49, 51, 60*t*, 97–98, 110–111, 124, 188

rates of development, 16, 29, 48, 52
See also Human genetic engineering
Genetic enhancement, 30–31, 49, 50, 159, 169
Genetic screening
cosmetic traits, 101, 102, 104–106, 108, 109, 110, 111–113
direct-to-consumer services and industry, 170–179, 181–186
diseases, 47, 54, 110, 112–113, 167, 168–169
and human genetic engineering, 47, 48, 101, 102
regulation, 170, 171, 177–179
Genetic transfer processes
crop breeding, 88–89, 98
rice, 85
Genetically engineered bacteria
energy products, 25
food products, 15–16
pharmaceutical products, 14, 27–28
Genetically engineered/modified food
animal production, 18, 29–30, 134–139, 140–144
could pose numerous health risks, 72–78, 97–98, 190–191
crop contamination, 34–36, 37, 187
have benefits and no known risks, 79–84, 90
information policies and manipulation, 73, 74, 75
labeling issues, 15, 18–19, 138–139, 155–156, 187–191, 190*t*, 192–197
lawsuits, 73, 196
prevalence, 15, 73, 87, 93, 188
public opinion, 18–19, 155–156, 188, 190*t*
See also Agricultural dilemmas; Agriculture; Plants
Genetically modified crops. *See* Agriculture
Genocides, 49, 162
Genomic data, consumer sales, 170–179, 181–186
Geoengineering, 121–122
Georgia, reproductive technology laws, 106, 113
Gerber, 80
Global power, 30, 159–160
Google, 171–172, 176
Graff, Gregory D., 83
Green, Ronald M., 46–52
"Green Revolution," 86–87
Greenhouse gas emissions
livestock sources, 122
market-based curbing attempts, 121
reduced, genetic engineering, 99–100, 116–117, 125–126
Greenpeace, 35, 117
Griswold v. Connecticut (1965), 168
Grocery Manufacturers of America, 35
Gurian-Sherman, Doug, 89–90

H

Haddock, 135
Halloran, Jean, 42–43, 45
Hansen, John, 38
Harkin, Tom, 44
Harl, Neil, 37, 43, 44
Hawaiian papaya, 24, 74, 76
Hayes, Richard, 56, 157–162

Health Canada, 149, 151
Health insurance, 177
Heinz, 80
Herbicides
crop tolerance and yields, 93, 94
genetically modified crop tolerance, 23–24, 74, 116, 117
volumes used, 117
HIV/AIDS treatment
biopharm drug development, 38, 41
gene therapy, 28–29, 70
Hochman, Gal, 83
Hormone treatments, humans, 123–125
Hormones
genetic engineering, food products, 15–16, 137
recombinant bovine somatotropin (rBST), 15–16, 154–156, 196
Hughes, Mark, 105
Human-animal hybrids, 55, 126–127, 166, 169
Human cloning, 65
international policies and relations, 159–160, 161*t*
opposition, 56, 57–62, 63, 159, 160, 166, 167
public opinion, 18, 159–160, 161
therapeutic cloning, 60*t*, 63, 66
Human Fertilisation and Embryology Authority (HFEA), 47, 164, 166, 168–169
Human genetic engineering
climate change mitigation tool, 119–128
climate change non-solution, 129–133
dangers, 48–49, 53–56, 101–107, 126–127
"enhancements," 30–31, 49, 50, 52, 169
human-animal hybrids, 55, 126–127, 166, 169
new technology does not need regulation, 163–169
new technology needs regulation, 157–162, 164–166, 167
should be allowed, 46–52
See also "Designer babies"
Human Genome Project, 21, 47–48, 172
Human nature, 127, 132
Human papillomavirus (HPV) vaccine, 27–28
Humans, physical size
environmental footprints, 119, 120, 123–126, 127, 130, 131, 133
genetic therapy or enhancements, 31, 159
Hunger
genetically engineered organisms, needs, 142
genetically modified crops can end, 85–91
genetically modified crops will not end, 92–100

I

In vitro fertilization (IVF)
international policies, 161*t*
regulation proposals, 165
research on effects, 50
usage and genetic selection, 47, 54, 104, 109, 123–124, 125

Indigenous agricultural systems, 26–27
Infertility
effect of GM foods, 73, 76–77
human reproductive therapies, 47, 50, 54, 104, 109, 113
Inflammatory arthritis, 15
Insecticides. *See* Pesticides and insecticides
Insects, beneficial, 117
Institute for Responsible Technology, 72–78
Insulin, development, 14, 27
Insulin-like growth factor 1 (IGF-1), 155
Insurance coverage, 177
Intelligence, enhancement, 30, 52, 111, 112, 169
International policies
direct-to-consumer genetic testing, 183, 184–185
food labeling, 189–190
genetic technologies, 47, 103, 107, 159, 161*t*, 166, 184–185
GM food import restrictions, 38
rBST bans, 16, 154, 155
International relations, 30, 159–160
International trade
genetically engineered pork, 150–151
genetically engineered seafood, 136, 137
genetically modified food, restrictions, 38
Interracial marriage, 168
Intrinsic yield, crop output, 94, 98

J

Japan
genetically modified food import restrictions, 38
rBST bans, 154
John Paul II (Pope), 52
Joy, Bill, 160

K

Kamrava, Michael, 102, 103, 104, 105
Kearns, William, 105
Kirin (brewer), 80
Knome (company), 173
Kyoto Protocol, 121

L

L-tryptophan, 77–78
Labeling. *See* Food labeling
Land use and agricultural productivity, 25, 26–27, 99, 195
Laos, Anthony, 35, 36, 41–42
Lateral gene transfer, 21
Lawler, Peter, 50
Leeder, Jessica, 142
Lenzer, Jeanne, 170–179
Leung, Wency, 142
Liao, S. Matthew, 119–128, 130–133
Liberty. *See* Freedom
Liss, Steven, 141, 144
Loving v. Virginia (1967), 168
Lurie, Peter, 178
Lynas, Mark, 53–56

M

Mackill, Dave, 88
Madsen, Pamela, 106
Maisto, Michelle, 193–194, 195, 196
Maize streak virus, 25
Marker-led plant breeding, 88–89, 89–90, 98
Marriage laws, 168
Maternal age, 103
McDonald's, 80
McKibben, Bill, 49, 55
Meat consumption
  decrease methods, and environmental benefits, 120, 122–123, 124, 126, 130
  genetically engineered pork, 140–144, 145–151
Medical records, 175–176
Merck (company), 27–28
Mexico, 86
Milk products, BST and rBST, 15–16, 154–156, 196
Miller, Henry I.
  criticism, genetic engineering activists, 82
  GM food labeling is unnecessary and unconstitutional, 192–197
  GM foods have benefits and no known risks, 79–84
Mims, Christopher, 181–186
Minard, Anne, 140–144
Monopolies, corporate, 24, 26
Monsanto (company)
  biopharming, 39–40, 41
  genetically modified foods funding, 88
  genetically modified foods information policy, 73, 74
  milk from rBST-treated cows, 155
Multiple births, 102, 103, 104, *104*, 105
Murdoch, Alison, 166

N

National Academy of Sciences, 23, 37
National Food Processors Association, 44
National Institutes of Health
  biopharming and research, 41
  bovine somatotropin food products policies, 16
  gene therapy projects, 28
  genomic research, 48
  ill-equipped to handle human genetic engineering, 165
Navigenics (company), 172, 178–179
Nazi Party, 49, 55, 162
New Zealand, rBST bans, 154
Nichols, John, 33–45
Norris, Chuck, 187–191
Nutritional improvements
  genetically engineered fruits, 25
  genetically engineered rice, 24, 26

O

Oakhurst Dairy, 155
Obama, Barack
  cloning policy, 57–62, 66
  genetically modified crops policy, 188
  stem cell research policy, 57–62, 64, 65–66

Obasogie, Osagie, 105
Obesity, genetics, 48
Obscenity laws, 168
Ocean health, 86, 100, 122, 141
Octuplets, 102, 103, 104, 105
Ontario Pork, 149
Operational yield, crop output, 94–95, 98
Organic farming
  crop contamination, 37, 187, 191
  research and development, 89–90
  used with genetically modified crop farming, 85, 87, 90, 99
Ornithine transcarbamylase deficiency (OTCD), 15
Overfishing, 135
Ozone layer, 122

P

Papaya, 24, 74, 76
Parent-child relationships
  death of a child, 54
  genetic engineering effects, 46, 49, 50, 51, 111
Personalized medicine
  direct-to-consumer genetic screening, 171–172, 173–174, 185–186
  pharmacogenomics, 175–176
Personhood debates, 106
Pest-resistant plants and crops (genetically engineered), 24, 25, 74, 81–82, 89, 93, 116, 117
Pesticides and insecticides
  agricultural productivity, 93, 94, 95
  agriculture use, 83, 86, 89, 90, 98
  bioaccumulation, 77, 117
  dangers to humans, 90
  reduced use/alternatives, 87, 89, 98–99, 116–117, 195
Pharmaceutical development
  crops and production dangers, 33–45
  history, genetic engineering, 14, 27
  human genetic engineering potential, 119, 120, 122–123, 124, 126, 130, 132
  pharmacogenomics, 175–176
Pharmaceutical prescriptions and predictions, 172–173
Pharmacogenomics, 175–176
Philippines, 86
Philips, John, 148
Phosphorus, in animal waste, 140, 141, 142, 143, 146, 147–148, 149
Phytase (enzyme), 142, 146
Pigs, genetically engineered, 140–144, 145–151
Plaice, 135
Plant viruses, 24, 25
Plants
  dangers of genetic engineering, 33–45, 74
  marker-led plant breeding, 88–89, 89–90, 98
  public opinion, genetic engineering, 18
  science opinion, genetic engineering, 22–23
  species grafting, 29
  targeted genetic engineering, 24–25, 74, 76, 90
"Playing God," 49, 52
Political categorization, 160, 162
Pollan, Michael, 87
Population growth, 26, 86, 142

Precautionary principle, 184–185
Preimplantation genetic diagnosis (PGD)
assisted reproductive technology and disease avoidance, 47, 54, 110, 112–113, 167, 168–169
assisted reproductive technology and trait selection, 47, 104–105, 109–111, 112, 169
assisted reproductive technology regulation, 165
genetic engineering: making humans smaller, 119, 123–124
risks, 167
Preventive medicine, 186
"Prisoner's dilemma," 158
Processed foods
genetically modified ingredients, 73, 194
recalls, 80–81
ProdiGene, 35, 36, 38–40, 41–42, 43
Productivity, agricultural
genetically modified crops do not increase, 92–100
genetically modified crops increase, 85–91
land use, 25, 26–27, 99, 195
US trends (non-GE), 95, 97
Prostate cancer, 173, 175
Public Citizen, 177
Public opinion, food labeling, 18–19, 155–156, 188, 190*t*
Public opinion, genetic engineering
demonstrations and protests, 22, 35
genetically engineered crops and food, 18–19, 97–100, 188
human genetic engineering and selection, 49, 51, 103, 108, 110–111, 159–160, 161
malleability, 124
scientists vs. public, 20, 22–23, 55
Public opinion, stem cell research, 57, 59
Public opinion, therapeutic cloning, 60*t*

R

Racial bias and genetic engineering, 105, 162
Random genetic mutation, 21–22
Recalls, products, 80–81
Recombinant bovine somatotropin (rBST), 15–16, 154–156
Recombinant DNA technology, 14, 81, 191
See also Genetically engineered/modified food
Reeve, Christopher, 62
Regulation
agriculture safety testing, 44, 98
biopharming: lacking and needed, 33, 35–36, 40, 42–44
cultural roadblocks, 160–161
direct-to-consumer genetic screening, 170, 171, 177–179, 181–186
gene therapy, 15, 159
genetically engineered animals, 137, 138, 144, 149–150
GM foods, 15, 16, 44, 73–74, 75, 190, 191

needed, new genetic engineering technology, 157–162
needed, reproductive and genetic medicine, 47, 101, 102–107, 164–166, 167
not needed, new genetic engineering technology, 163–169
not needed, reproductive and genetic medicine, 108–113
overregulation complaints, 83, 166, 183, 184
prevention, 55
rBST, 15, 154–156
society unequipped for human engineering, 53, 55, 106–107, 158–162, 165
stem cell research, 60, 165, 166, 167
"voluntary," 40, 43

Religious concerns
cloning, 56, 160
human genetic engineering, 49, 52
stem cell research, 56

Reproductive cloning. *See* Human cloning

"Reprogenetics," 47

Research
crop productivity, 93–100
funding, 88, 89–90, 98
gene therapy and disease treatment, 14–15, 70–71
genetically engineered crops, 24–25, 37, 41, 44–45, 82–83, 87–89, 89–90, 93–100
genetically engineered weapons, 160
genomic sequencing, 47–48
in-vitro fertilization outcomes, 50
needed, GM foods, 73, 74, 75, 78
needed, organics, 89–90
neuro-degenerative diseases, 55
pharmaceutical drugs, 173
stem cells (opposition), 63–67
stem cells (support), 57–62, 166
therapeutic cloning, 60*t*, 66, 167

Reynolds, Jesse, 101–107

Rice
biopharming, 40
flood and climate protections, 85, 88–89
global consumption, 87–88
high-yield, 85, 86, 90
nutritional improvements, 24, 26

Ringspot virus, 24

Ritchie, Mark, 36–37

Roache, Rebecca, 121, 124, 132–133

Roe v. Wade (1973), 168

Rogers, Jim, 35–36

Ronald, Pam, 87–91

Russia, 160

Ryan, Jennalee, 54

S

Safeway, 155

Saletan, William, 113

Salmon, 135, 136, 137, 138–139

Salt tolerance, 24, 25

Samaha, Simon, 176–177

Sandberg, Anders, 121, 124, 132–133

Satel, Sally, 50

Scientific Committee on Animal Health and Animal Welfare (European Commission), 154–155
Scientific Committee on Veterinary Measures Relating to Public Health (European Commission), 155
Scientific freedom, 61
Sea level rises, 99
Self-regulation, "voluntary"
- biopharming and GE crops, 40, 43
- fertility industry, 101, 102–103, 110

Sex selection, 110, 165, 166, 168
Sharratt, Lucy, 145–151
Single nucleotide polymorphisms (SNPs), 171, 173
Skin cell stem cells, 64, 66
Skin color, 105
Smith, Jeffrey M., 75
Society for Assisted Reproductive Technology, 103
Soy
- agricultural productivity, 93–95, 97, 98–99
- allergies, 74–75, 76
- biopharming and contamination, 34–35, 36, 40
- genetically engineered, 15, 23–24, 34–35, 40, 73, 74–75, 76–77, 93–95, 97, 99, 116–117, 188

Speciation, 49
Starbucks, 155
State laws
- antidiscrimination, 177
- embryo screening and selection, 106–107, 112, 113
- eugenics, 168
- genetic modifications, labeling, 191, 196

Steinberg, Jeffrey, 104–105, 106, 109–111
Stem cell research
- ethical and moral opposition, 56, 63–67, 106, 167
- international policies, 161*t*, 166
- new technologies and processes, 165
- should be allowed, but not for cloning, 57–62, 167
- skin cells, 64, 66
- stem cell types, 64

Stephan, Dietrich, 178–179
Sterilization, forced, 49, 168
Sugar beets, 74
Sulston, John, 178
Sundberg, Paul, 144
Sunshine Project, 160
Supplements, 189, 190
Surveillance bias, 175, 176
Surveys
- genetic engineering, 18–19
- new human genetic technologies, 161
- therapeutic cloning, 60*t*

Sustainability
- agricultural productivity, 25, 26–27, 85–91, 99–100
- fishing, 135, 139
- genetic engineering offerings, 22
- human genetic engineering as tool, 119–128

T

Tapson, Mark, 129–133
Tarne, Gene, 65

Taylor, Michael, 73
Technology development
new genetic engineering technology doesn't need regulation, 163–169
new genetic engineering technology needs regulation, 101–107, 157–162
weighing risks, 70, 158–159, 162
Therapeutic cloning, 60*t*, 63, 66, 161*t*, 167
Tobacco, 40
Tomorrow's Table (Ronald), 87
Trade. *See* International trade
Traditional agricultural methods, 26–27, 98, 99
"Tragedy of the commons," 158
Trait selection. *See* "Designer babies"
Transparency issues, GM crops and food, 42, 75, 149–150
Tumor suppressor genes, 27–28
Tuna, 135
23andMe (company), 171–172, 172–173, 174, 175, 176, 183

U

Undifferentiated pluripotent stem cells, 64
Union of Concerned Scientists, 89, 92–100
United Kingdom
regulation standards: consumer genetic testing, 178
regulation standards: PGD and reproductive technologies, 47, 103, 107, 159, 163, 166, 168–169
United Nations
bioweapons policies, 160
Food and Agriculture Organization codes, 188–189
Food and Agriculture Organization data, 122, 135, 137, 142
GE foods policies, 99
and United States, genetic engineering, 187–191
United States
cloning policies, 160
regulation history, 106–107, 163, 164, 168
and United Nations, genetic engineering, 187–191
See also US Department of Agriculture (USDA); US Food and Drug Administration (FDA)
University of Guelph, 141, 143, 146, 148, 149–150
US Department of Agriculture (USDA)
agricultural productivity data, 95–96, 97
Animal and Plant Health Inspection Service, 35–36
biopharm regulations needs, 42–43, 44
deregulation targets, 190, 191
food labeling, 189–190, 195–196
genetic engineering data, 23–24
US Food and Drug Administration (FDA)
biopharm regulations needs, 42, 44
biopharming approvals, 39–40
consumer genetic testing, 178–179, 182–184, 186

food labeling, 155–156, 189–190
gene therapy oversight, 15
genetically engineered animals/foods, 137, 138, 144
GM foods approvals, 15, 16, 73–74, 75
ill-equipped to handle human genetic engineering, 165
rBST oversight, 16, 154–156
support of genetic engineering, 14
US Supreme Court, cases, 168

V

Vaccine development
biopharming crops, 38–39, 40, 41
human papillomavirus (HPV), 27–28
Vance, Erik, 85–91
Vegetarianism, 120, 122–123, 124, 130
Veneman, Ann, 44
Vertically integrated businesses, 148
Vilsack, Tom, 41
Viral DNA, 21, 73, 74
Virginia, Loving v. (1967), 168
Vision correction, 28, 30, 126–127, 130–131
Vitamin and mineral supplements, 189, 190
Vogel, Sarah, 42

W

Wade, Roe v. (1973), 168
Wald, George, 190–191
Walmart, 155
Warren, Rick, 65–66
Water pollution
agricultural runoff, 141, 143, 146, 147, 148
oceans, 86, 100, 141
Weapons development and treaties, 160
Weather, as contamination factor, 43, 45
Welch, Gilbert, 174, 175, 176
Wheat, 25, 86, 90, 97
White House Office of Science and Technology Policy, 61
Wojcicki, Anne, 174, 176
Woods, Tiger, 51
World Health Organization (WHO)
bovine somatotropin food products policies, 16
codes, 188–189

X

X-linked severe combined immunodeficiency (X-SCID), 15, 70–71

Z

Zilberman, David, 83
Zohar, Yonathan, 134–139